j612.8

THE HUMAN MACHINE

THE
CONTROLS

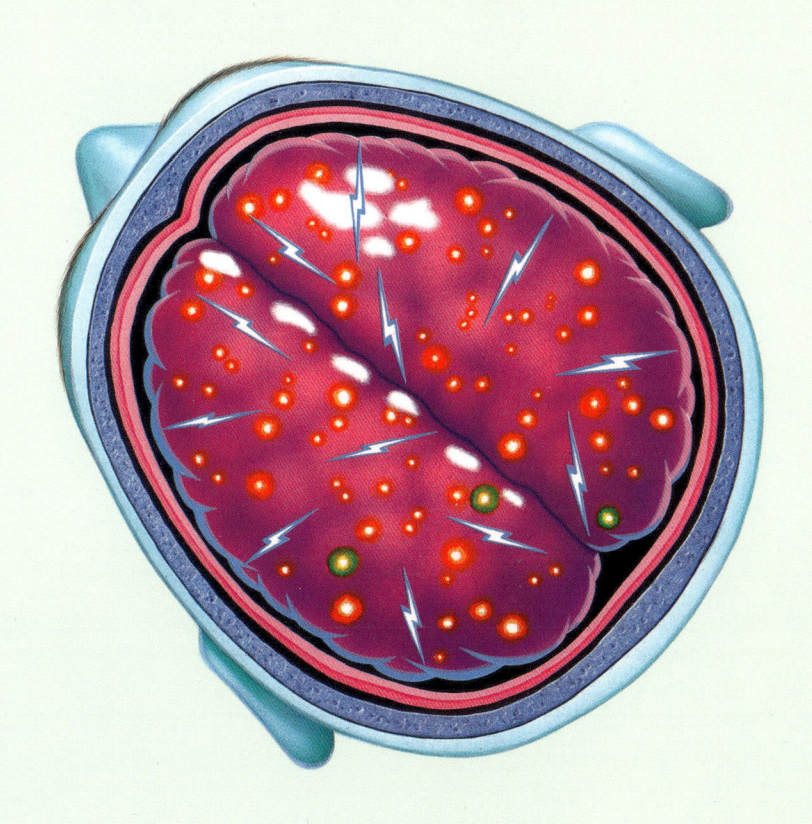

Sarah Angliss

Illustrations by Tom Connell

Thameside Press

U.S. publication copyright © 2000 Thameside Press.
International copyright reserved in all countries.
No part of this book may be reproduced in any
form without written permission from the publisher.

Distributed in the United States by
Smart Apple Media
123 South Broad Street
Mankato, Minnesota 56001

Text copyright © Sarah Angliss 2000

Editor: Susie Brooks
Designer: Helen James
Educational consultant: Carol Ballard

Printed in Singapore

ISBN 1-929298-22-6
Library of Congress Catalog Card Number 99-66190

10 9 8 7 6 5 4 3 2 1

Words in **bold** are explained in the glossary on pages 30 and 31.

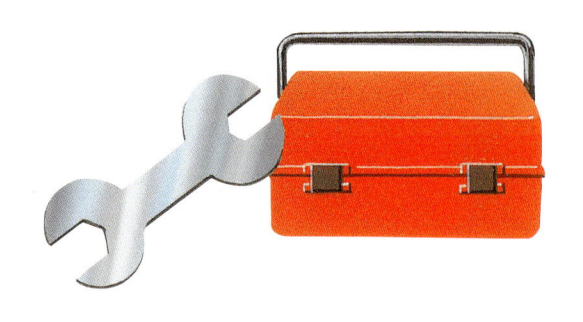

CONTENTS

The Controls About this book **4**

Electric Jelly Skull and brain **6**

Control Connections Brain and neurons **8**

Wiring Up Spinal cord and nerve network **10**

Ticking Over Hypothalamus and autonomic nerves **12**

Light Sensors Eyes and sight **14**

Mini Microphones Ears and hearing **16**

Chemical Testers Taste and smell **18**

Fine Feelers Touch and pain **20**

Information Exchange Cerebral hemispheres **22**

Specialist Sections Thalamus and divisions of cortex **24**

Care and Servicing Looking after your brain **26**

Other Models Brain and senses of other animals **28**

Glossary **30**

Index **32**

THE CONTROLS

Think of your body as an amazing machine—a human machine. It can do so many things because it has a complex set of controls—your nervous system. Your brain, nerves, and sensors keep a check on your body and its surroundings, making you think, feel, and move as things around you change.

Control center

Your brain is your control center. Although it's no bigger than a grapefruit, it is more complicated than any other machine we know. Your brain is packed with billions of tiny **cells**, called **neurons**, that are linked together in a tangled network. It works by sending electrical pulses between these cells.

Long bundles of **fibers**, called **nerves**, run all around your body. Your brain uses these to keep in touch with other body parts.

Signal system

Your brain needs to know what's going on around you, so it can decide, from moment to moment, what you should do. That's why you have your **sense organs**—body parts that contain tiny cells called **receptors**. These cells react to changes in and around your body. They send messages along nerves to your brain, keeping it up to date. Together, your brain, nerves, and sense organs make up your **nervous system**.

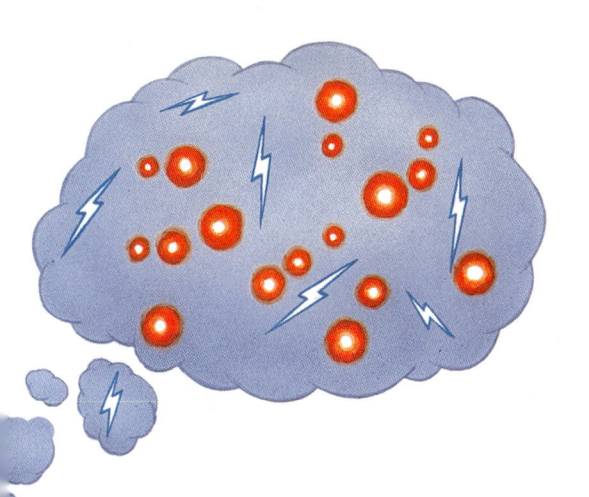

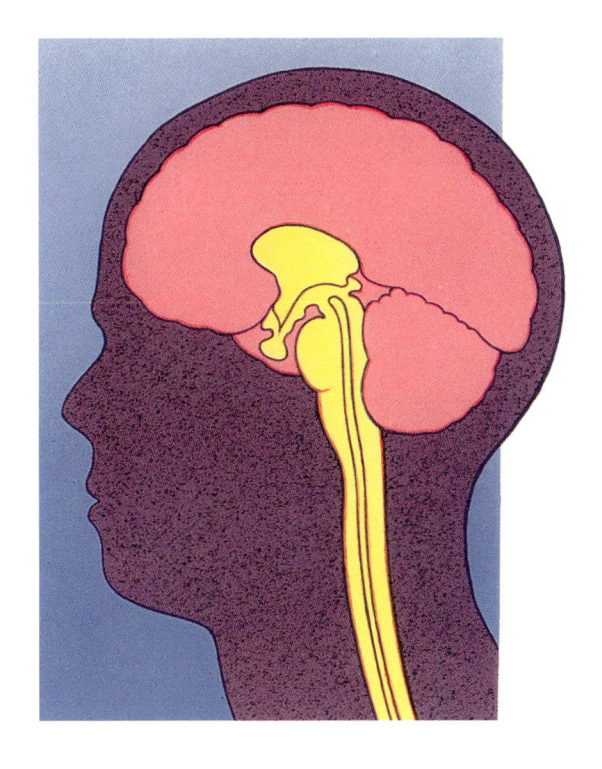

Gray area

We're only just beginning to grasp how the brain and the rest of the nervous system work together to run a human machine. As we discover more about them, we learn how we can run, see, feel, speak, imagine, make decisions—and do everything else that makes us human. If you didn't have a brain, you wouldn't be able to read this book!

Look out for pictures like the one above throughout this book. They show you where each part of your control system is found in your body. Other small diagrams show what some of these parts really look like.

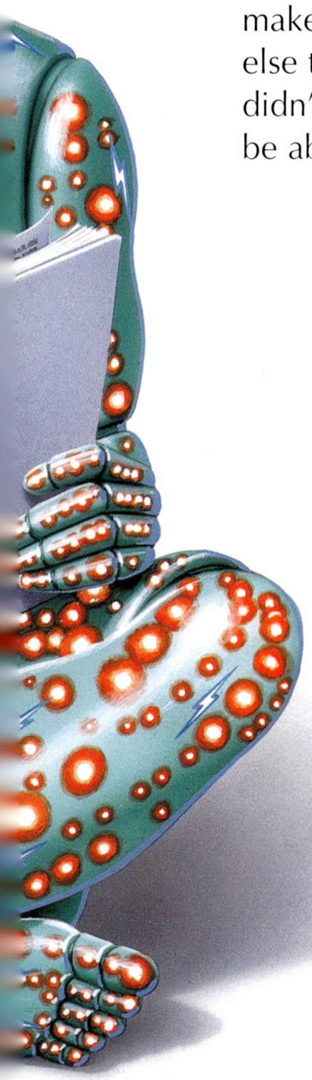

Weird wires

Your nervous system isn't really made of jelly, wires, and lights! The main pictures in this book were drawn with a little imagination. But look at each one carefully—they show how your controls work.

Breakdown!

Just like any other piece of machinery, the human controls need to be handled with care. But no matter how well you look after them, parts of your nervous system can sometimes go wrong. Toolboxes like this one show you how some parts can break down—and how they may be repaired.

ELECTRIC JELLY

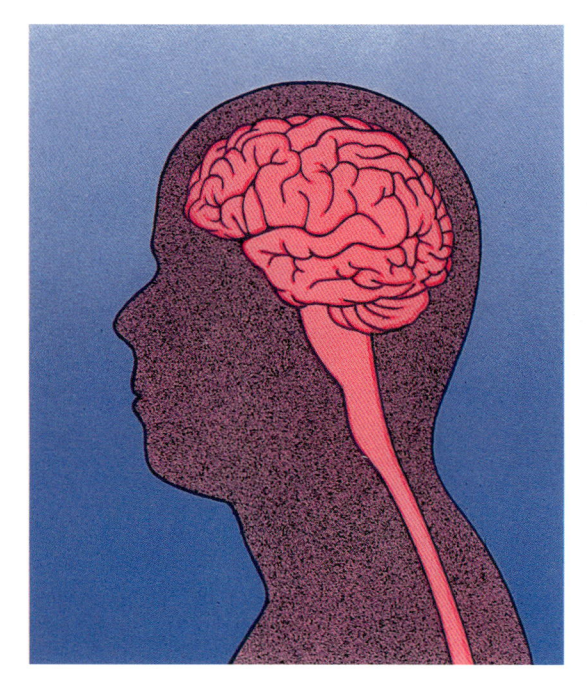

Your brain may look like a lifeless mound of jelly, but it is actually active day and night. Billions of neurons work together to create your thoughts and memories and to control how the rest of your body works.

Just like a computer, your brain runs using electricity. But that's where the similarity ends. You can shut down a computer at the end of the day, for example, but your brain never switches off completely—even when you're asleep.

Brain box

Your brain is very delicate, so it needs plenty of protection. That's why it's enclosed in a hard case —your skull. Inside this bony box, three skin-like layers wrap around your brain. Between them is a watery fluid that acts like a shock-absorber, cushioning your brain against bumps.

If you lifted the top off your skull, you'd see a large, wrinkled lump, split down the middle into two halves. This is your **cerebrum** —the biggest part of your brain.

What happens in your cerebrum? Find out on pages 22–25.

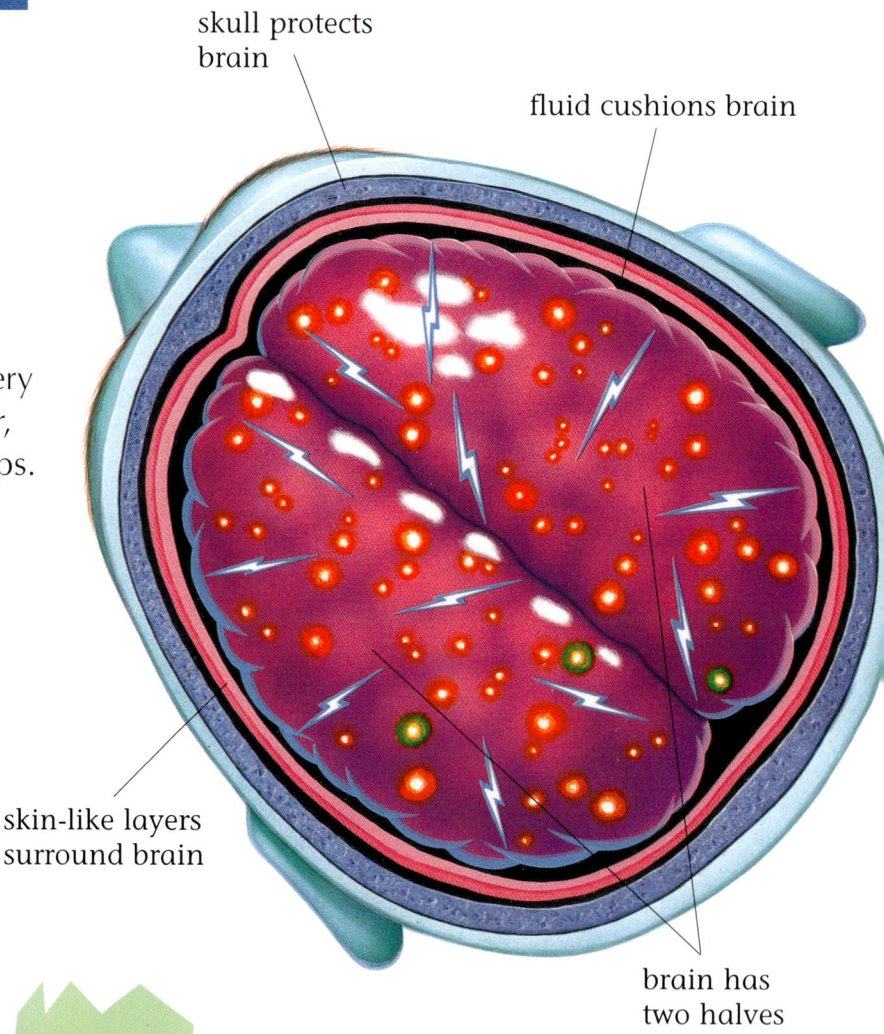

skull protects brain

fluid cushions brain

skin-like layers surround brain

brain has two halves

Packed in

If you could have a close look at your cortex, you'd see that it's full of wrinkles. Flattened out, it would be about the size of a pillowcase. Its wrinkles enable the whole thing to be packed into the small space inside your head.

Cross-section through the brain

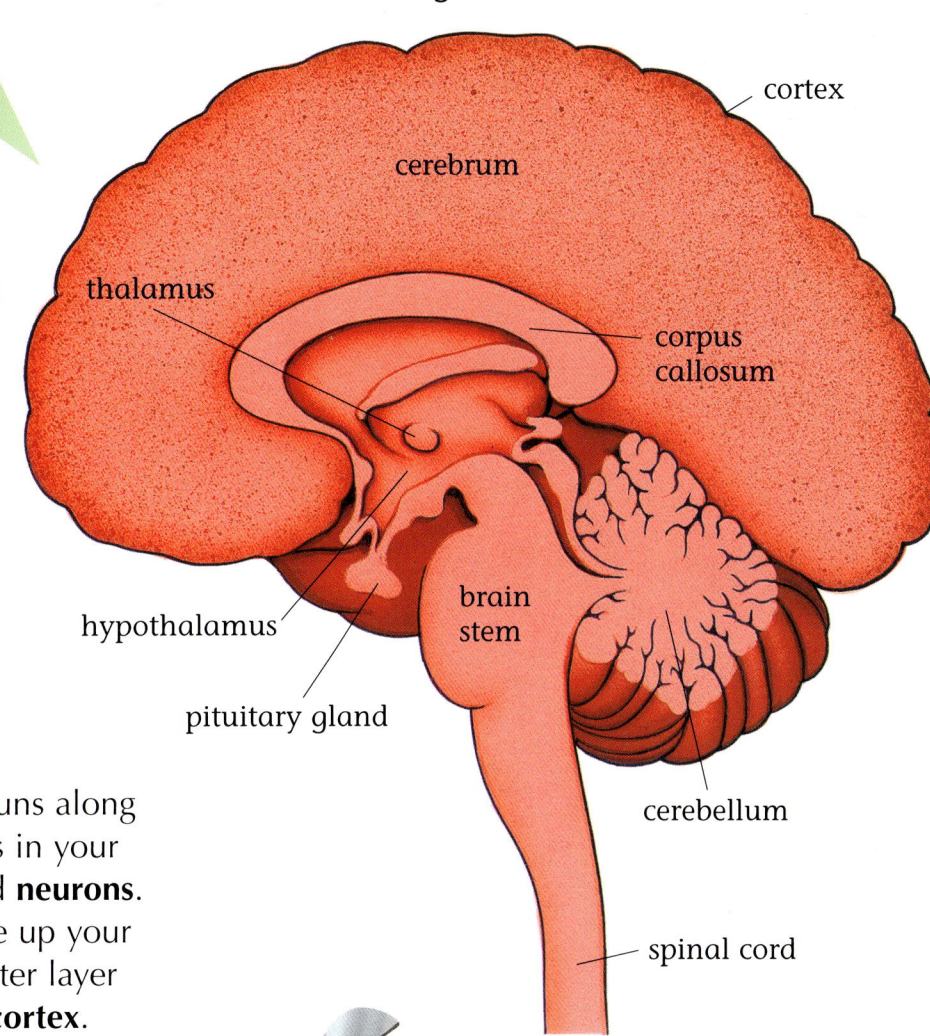

- cortex
- cerebrum
- thalamus
- corpus callosum
- hypothalamus
- pituitary gland
- brain stem
- cerebellum
- spinal cord

Cell center

The electricity in your home runs along wires. But the electrical pulses in your brain flow through **cells** called **neurons**. The bodies of these cells make up your **gray matter**. This forms the outer layer of your cerebrum, called the **cortex**.

Neurons are linked together by long **fibers**. Many of these are bundled under your cortex, forming your **white matter**. Neurons and their fibers are surrounded by other brain cells called **neuroglia**. These look after your neurons, but they don't generate electrical pulses.

Brain bits

At the base and core of your brain there are several other regions which have very special functions. Some of these are labeled in the diagram above. You can find out why you need each brain area as you read the rest of this book.

Mind benders

Your brain is fueled by **oxygen** and **nutrients**. These are carried in your blood, which flows to your brain along tiny tubes called **capillaries**. Gaps in your capillary walls allow these fuels to seep into your brain. But some other chemicals, such as alcohol and **anesthetics**, may also leak through. That's why they can affect the way you feel.

CONTROL CONNECTIONS

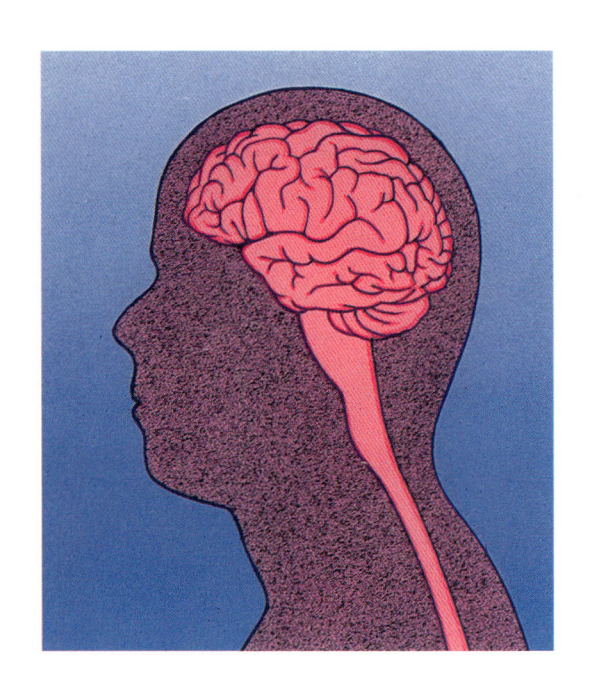

The human brain is far less orderly than a computer. The fibers that join your neurons form a messy tangle, like a rat's nest of wires.

Clever chaos

The billions of **neurons** that make up your brain can send messages in countless billions of different patterns. Every pattern helps to create a different thought, action, feeling, or memory.

Amazingly, it's the untidiness of your brain that helps it to work so well. If your neurons were joined together in a much neater network, they would be able to work in far fewer ways.

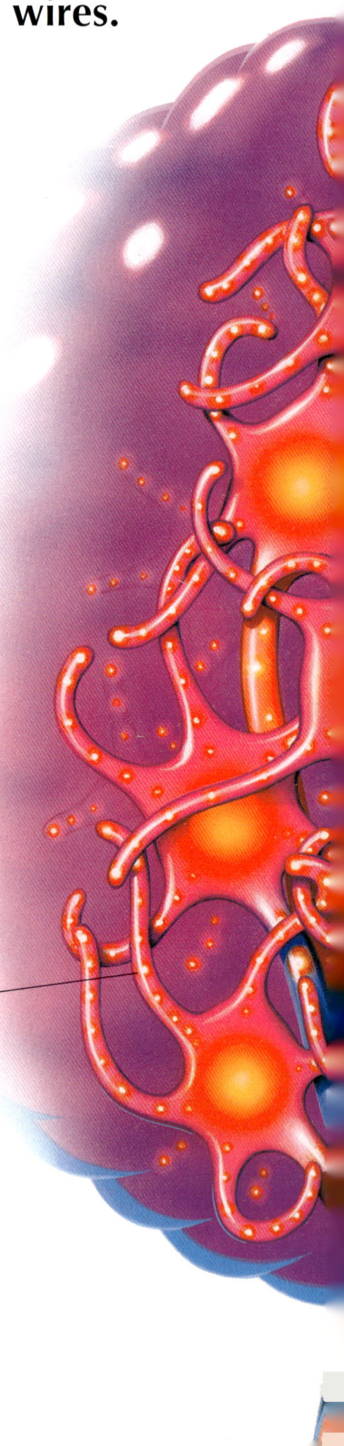

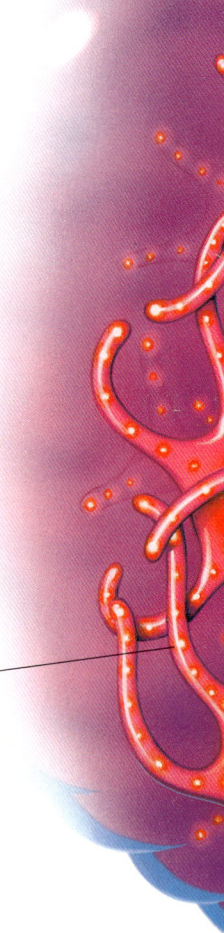

dendrites receive pulses from other cells

Feeling fuzzy

Alcohol and other **sedative** drugs make it much harder for messages to jump from one neuron to another. That's why they make us feel numb and sleepy. When you are overtired, your body may also be short of the chemicals your brain needs to send messages. That's why it's usually easiest to think or do difficult things after a good night's sleep.

Mind messages

Most neurons in your brain have at least two **fibers**, called **dendrites**, that bring in messages from other **cells**. They also have one longer fiber, called an **axon**, that can pass on messages to other cells. The body of a neuron monitors the messages that move along its dendrites, and decides when to send a pulse to another cell.

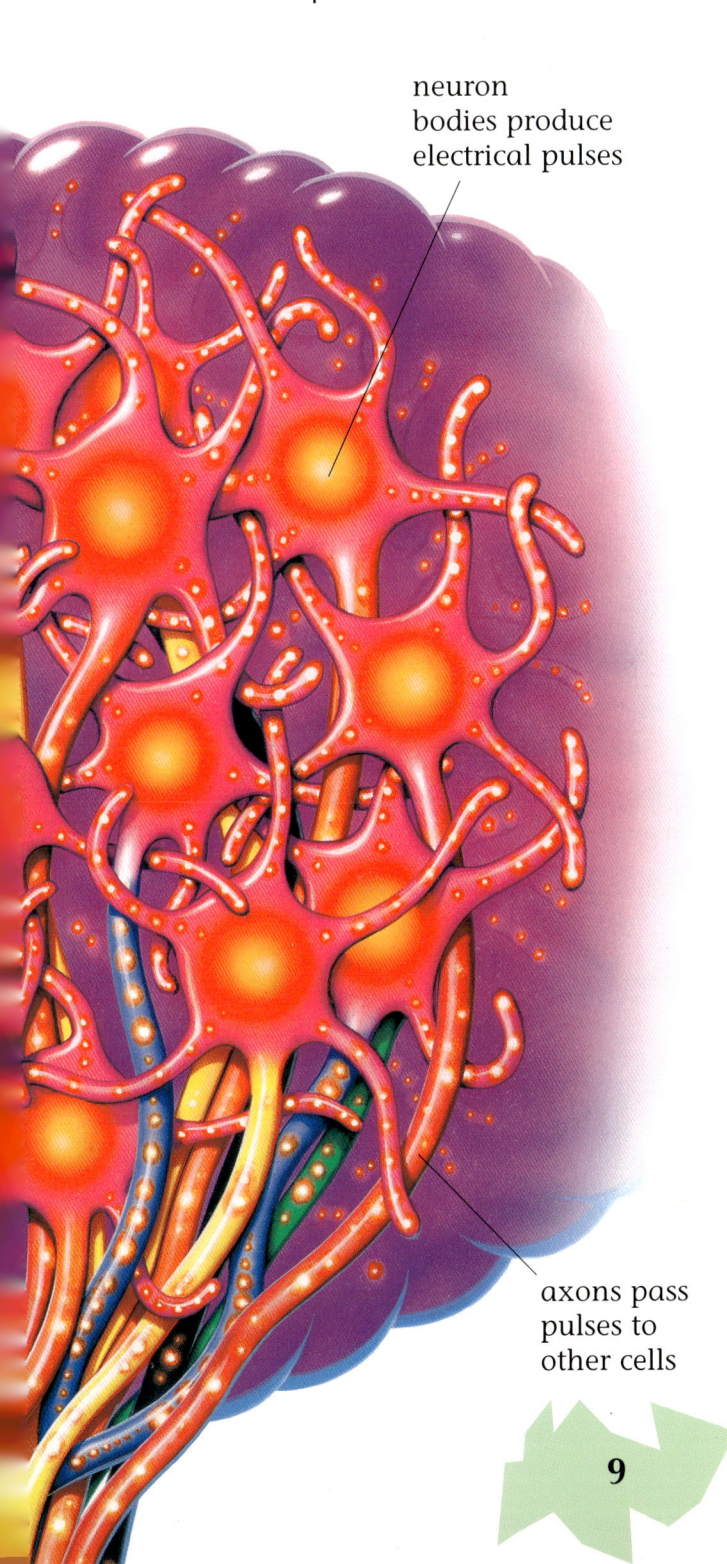

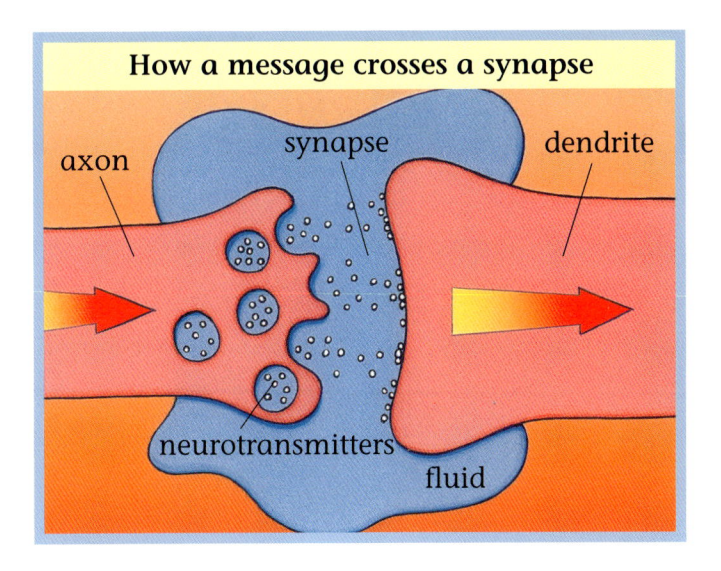

neuron bodies produce electrical pulses

How a message crosses a synapse

axon — synapse — dendrite
neurotransmitters
fluid

Bridging the gap

Nerve fibers don't join together properly where they meet—there's a gap between them called the **synapse**. This gap is filled with a fluid which sloshes around the end of each fiber. Messages flow from one fiber to another when the axon of one cell squirts chemicals called **neurotransmitters** into the fluid. If it squirts enough, these chemicals will be soaked up by the end of a nearby dendrite. This will trigger an electrical pulse to flow through it into the receiving cell.

Permanent practice

Unlike an ordinary computer circuit, the connections in your brain aren't fixed for life. New ones are made every time you try out different things. If you practice something, such as riding a bike or remembering a friend's telephone number, the new connections may become permanent. That's why you're often able to keep a skill or store a memory for life.

axons pass pulses to other cells

WIRING UP

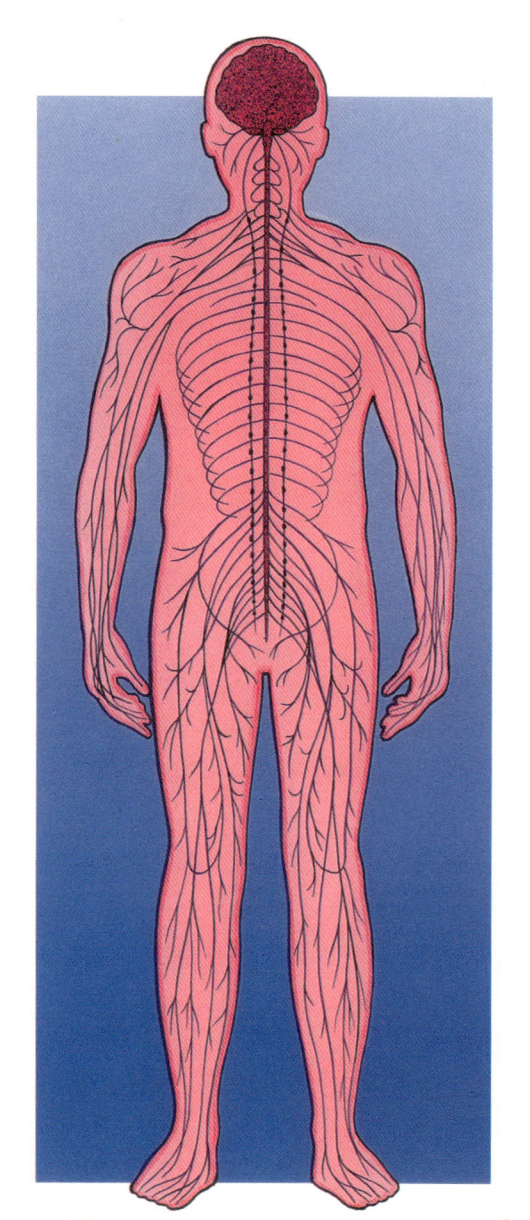

Your brain keeps in touch with the rest of your body through a network of nerves. These act like the wires between rooms in a building. They let electrical pulses move to and from almost every other part of your body.

sensory nerves carry signals to brain

bony spine protects spinal cord

Bundle of nerves

The thousands of **nerves** that trail through your body come together to form a neat cable which runs up your spine and into your brain. This is your **spinal cord**. The center of your spinal cord is made up of **gray matter**. The outer part is mainly **white matter**.

Thirty-one pairs of nerves branch off your spinal cord, to the left and right sides of your body. These split into even finer branches that reach out to every body part from your neck downward. Your head has its own nerve network that plugs directly into your brain.

Long and short

As nerve **fibers** have to run to different parts of your body, some are much longer than others. The neurons in your brain, for example, have fibers that are microscopic in length. But your longest nerves, running from your spinal cord to the bottom of your leg, can be well over a yard long.

Two-way traffic

Your **nervous system** works in two directions. **Sensory nerves** carry messages to your brain from **receptors**—cells that pick up changes in your body or the world around it. **Motor nerves** carry messages in the opposite direction. They enable your brain to tell other body parts what to do.

motor nerves carry signals from brain

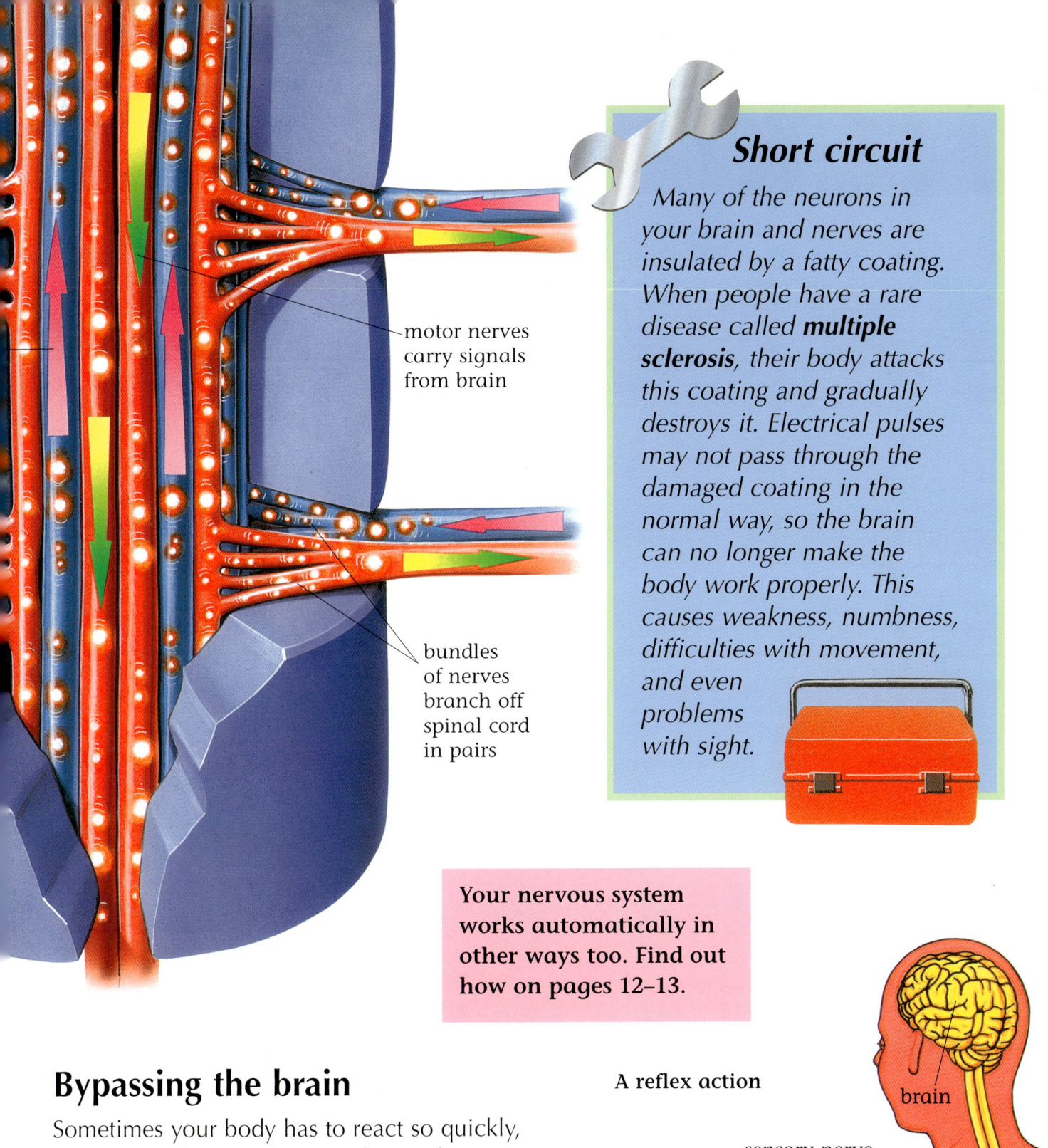

bundles of nerves branch off spinal cord in pairs

Short circuit

Many of the neurons in your brain and nerves are insulated by a fatty coating. When people have a rare disease called **multiple sclerosis**, their body attacks this coating and gradually destroys it. Electrical pulses may not pass through the damaged coating in the normal way, so the brain can no longer make the body work properly. This causes weakness, numbness, difficulties with movement, and even problems with sight.

Your nervous system works automatically in other ways too. Find out how on pages 12–13.

Bypassing the brain

Sometimes your body has to react so quickly, it can't wait for signals to reach your brain. When you touch something very hot, for example, you automatically pull your hand away. That's because receptors in your skin flash messages along nerves to your spinal cord. **Neurons** in the spinal cord pick up these messages and send back an instant response to your body muscles. This is called a **reflex** action.

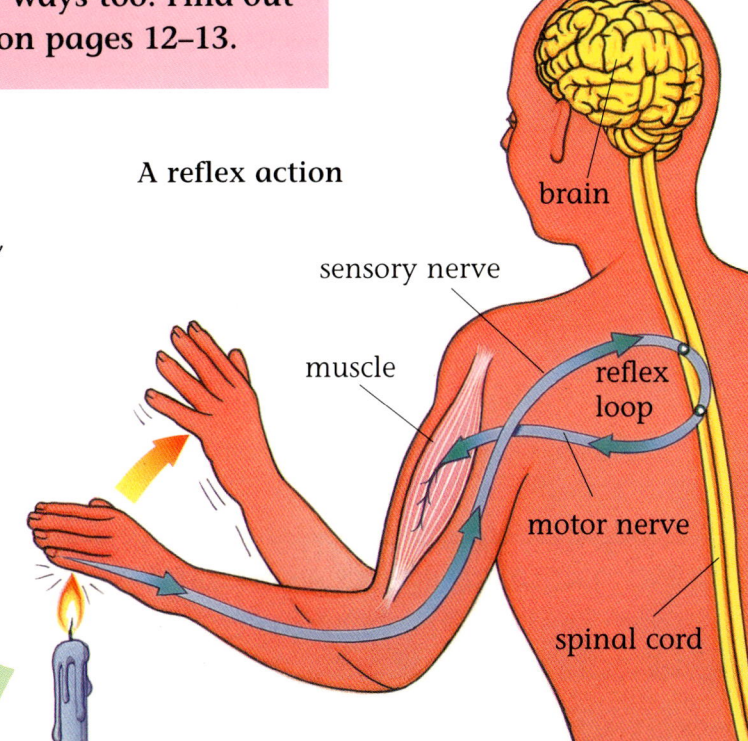

A reflex action

brain
sensory nerve
muscle
reflex loop
motor nerve
spinal cord

11

TICKING OVER

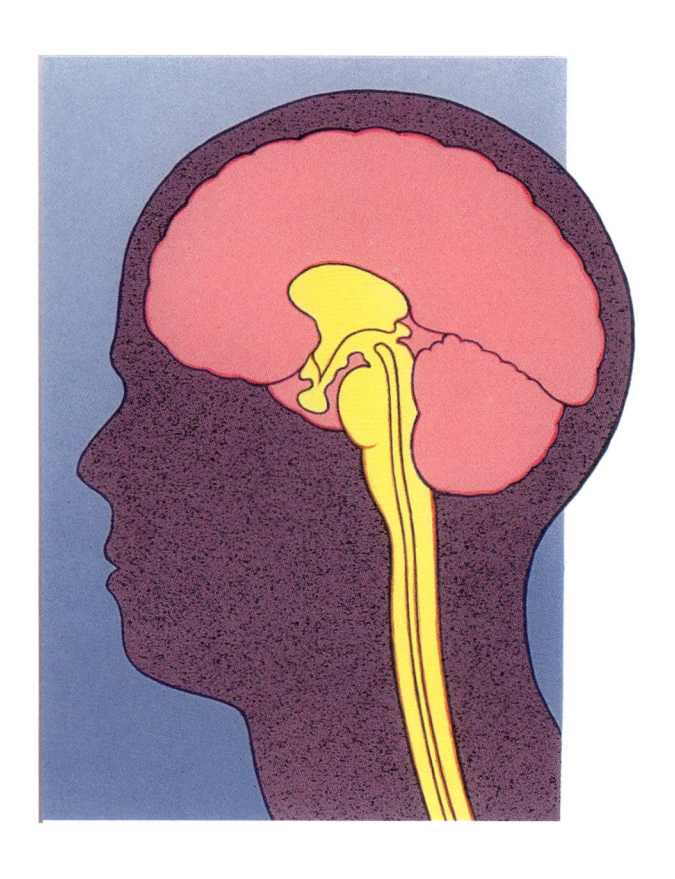

Your nervous system has a special set of controls that enables your body to run on automatic. This saves your brain from being overloaded.

Your body has plenty to do to keep you alive. Your heart, for instance, has to beat, and your lungs have to take in air. Luckily your **nervous system** can control these tasks, without you having to think about them most of the time.

On automatic

The network that's in charge of your body's automatic actions is called your **autonomic nervous system**. It's made up of two sets of **nerves** that work together to make sure your body parts run smoothly all the time.

Super stem

Parts of your autonomic nervous system are controlled by **gray matter** in or around your **spinal cord**. But your body's main autopilot is your **brain stem**. This stalk at the base of your brain controls many of the actions that keep you alive. It's also in charge of some **reflexes**, for instance the one that makes your **pupils** shrink when a bright light shines into your eyes.

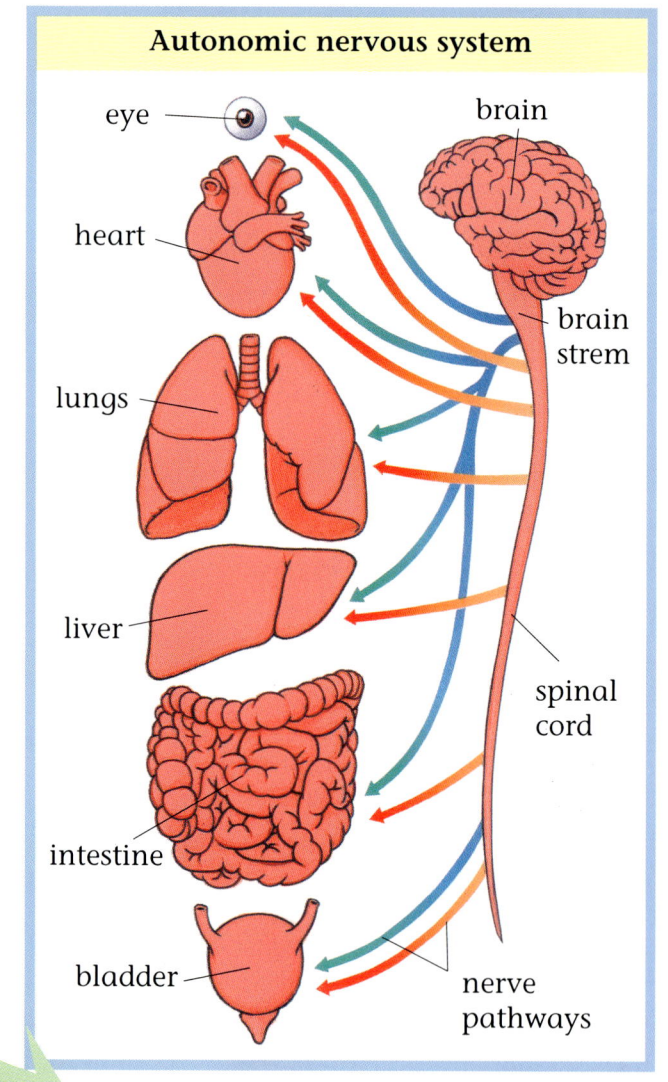

Autonomic nervous system

eye — brain — heart — lungs — liver — intestine — bladder — brain stem — spinal cord — nerve pathways

pituitary gland makes hormones

hypothalamus monitors body changes

hypothalamus sends signals telling body parts what to do

nerves carry signals about changes in body

Keeping constant

Just above your brain stem is your body's main regulator—your **hypothalamus**. This constantly monitors body functions such as your heart rate, temperature, sleepiness, and hunger. If it senses any changes, it sends out signals to put you right. Some of these are carried by your autonomic nervous system. Other signals trigger the nearby **pituitary gland** to send out special chemical messengers called **hormones**.

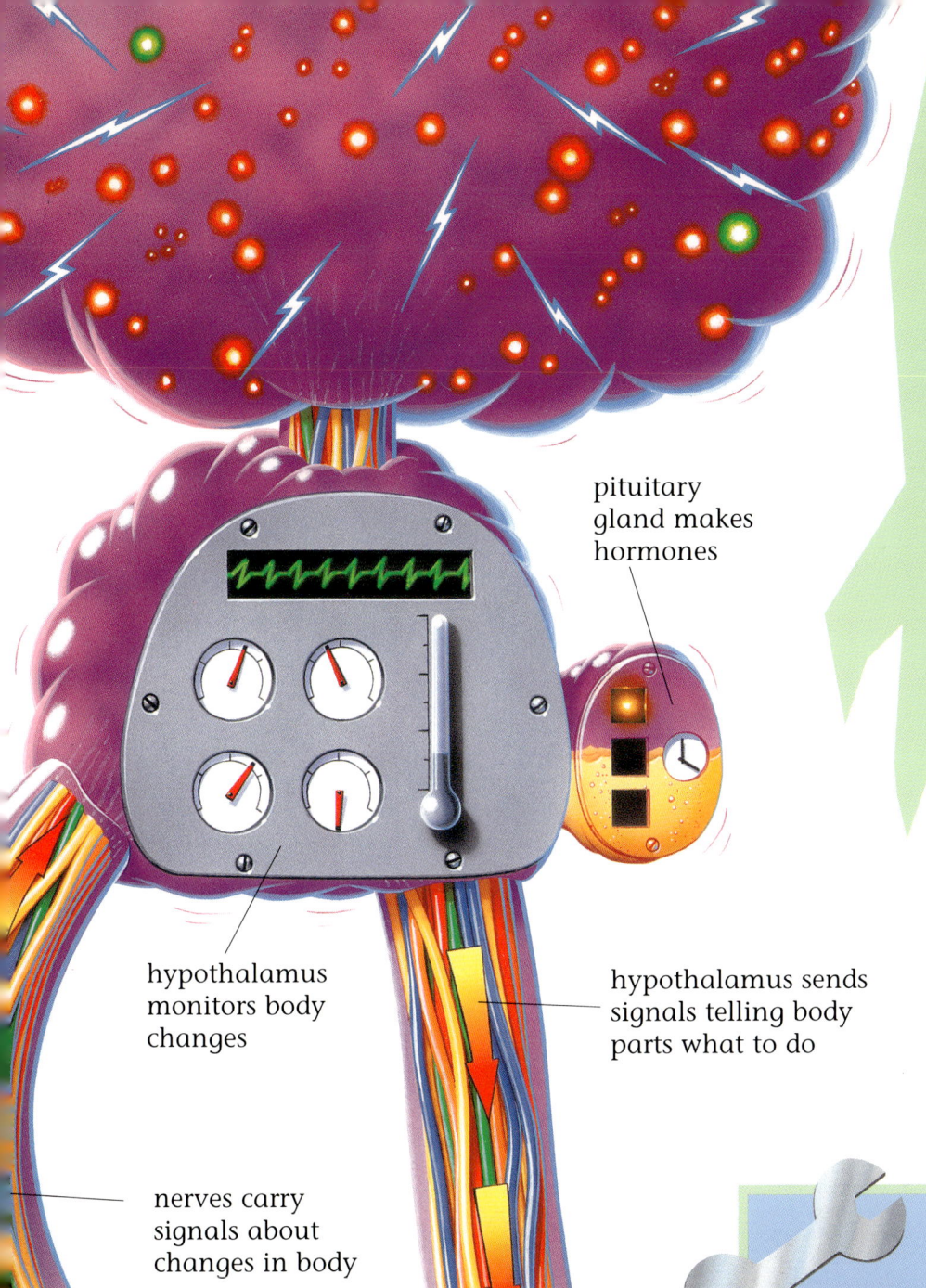

Fight or flight

Some nerves immediately go into action when you're frightened. They gear you up to deal with, or escape from, the danger at hand. For example, they make your heart beat faster and pump more blood into your legs so you're ready to run. When the danger has gone, other nerves act automatically. They undo these changes, gradually calming you down.

What else does your brain stem do? Find out on pages 22–23.

Too wound up

The nerves that help you deal with danger can go to work even when something isn't life-threatening. They may make you feel anxious just before an exam, for example. If people have to deal with situations like this too often, their bodies may not have time to fully calm down. They may end up suffering from stress. This can make them tired and ill.

LIGHT SENSORS

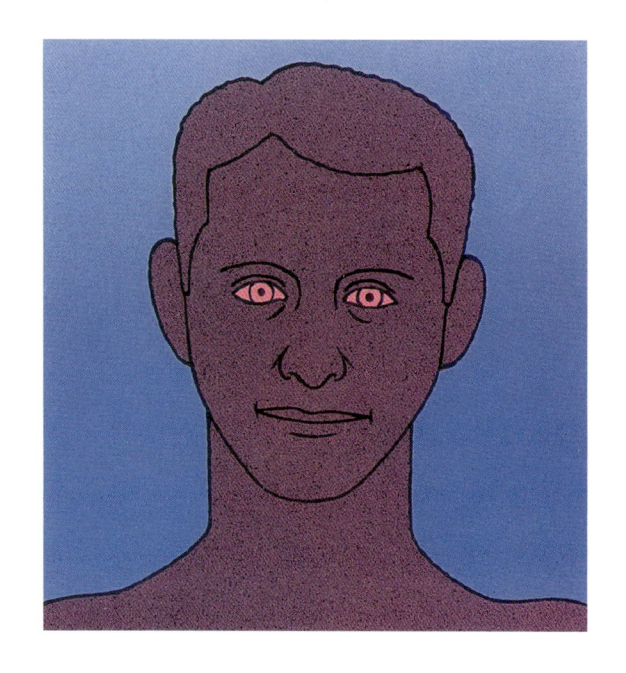

The face of the human machine has two built-in cameras—your eyes. These ball-shaped sense organs send messages to your brain whenever light rays shine on them.

Your eyes are connected to your brain by two bundles of **neurons** called **optic nerves**. Your brain uses messages from your eyes to let you see and make sense of the world around you.

Picture perfect

Each eye works like a simple camera. The dark circle at the center, called the **pupil**, is an opening that lets in rays of light. When light shines through, **receptors** at the back of your eye send messages to your brain. Billions of brain **cells** process these messages. They make you aware of the scene in front of you and enable you to work out what it is.

brain tells you what you're seeing

optic nerves carry signals

Shutter control

A ring of muscle around your pupil opens and closes as the brightness of light reaching your eye changes. This muscle, called your **iris**, acts like a shutter, adjusting the amount of light that's coming in. The size of your iris is controlled by **reflexes**.

Find out more about reflexes on pages 11–13.

In-depth vision

You need both eyes to work together, or you'd find it very difficult to judge distances. As your eyes are set a couple of inches apart, they each pick up a slightly different image of the world around you. Your brain works out the difference between the two images to tell how far away things are.

Rods and cones on the retina

cone

nerve fiber

rod

Liquid lens

The eyeball is anchored to tiny muscles that are controlled by reflexes. Some of these let you move your eyes around. Other muscles squash or stretch a sack of liquid, called the **lens**, making it fatter or thinner. This bends light rays more or less so you can see things that are nearer or further away.

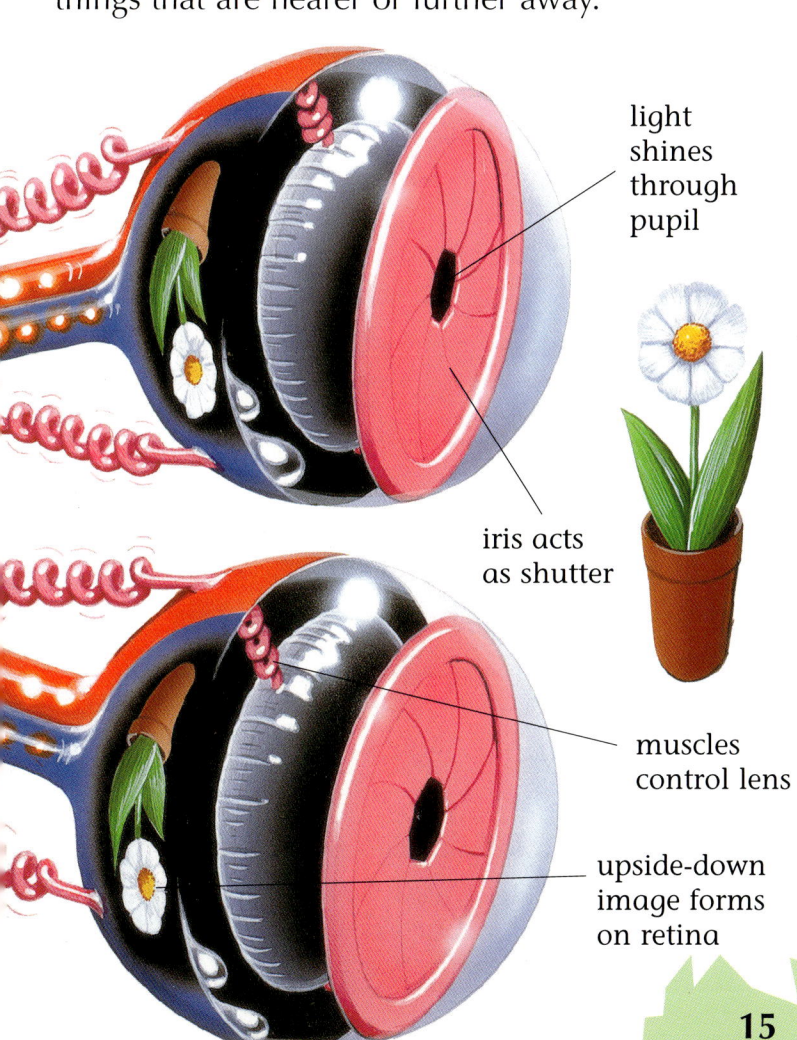

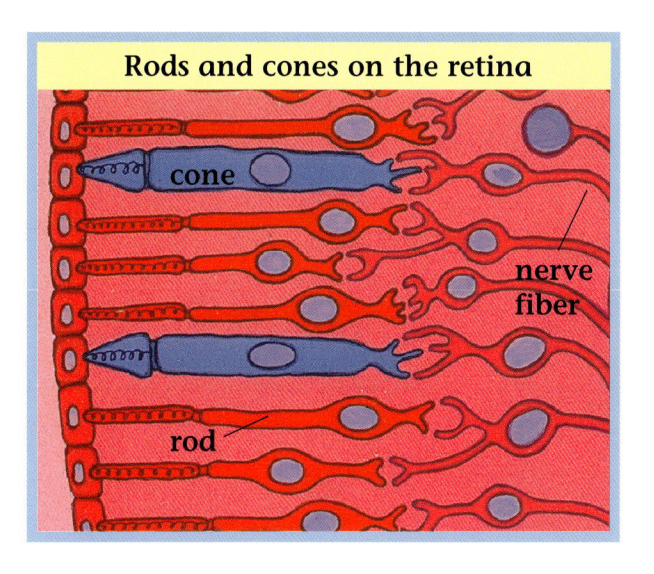

Rods and cones

Around three-quarters of your body's receptors are packed into your eyes. They cover the lining at the back of each eyeball, called the **retina**. Some receptors are rod-shaped. They work even in dim light, helping you to see shades of gray. The others, which are cone-shaped, only work in brighter light. These give you your color sight.

light shines through pupil

iris acts as shutter

muscles control lens

upside-down image forms on retina

Color cross

Some people have a problem with the cone-shaped receptors lining their eyes. This makes them color blind—unable to tell certain colors apart. Most color blind people find it difficult to tell the difference between red and green.

15

MINI-MICROPHONES

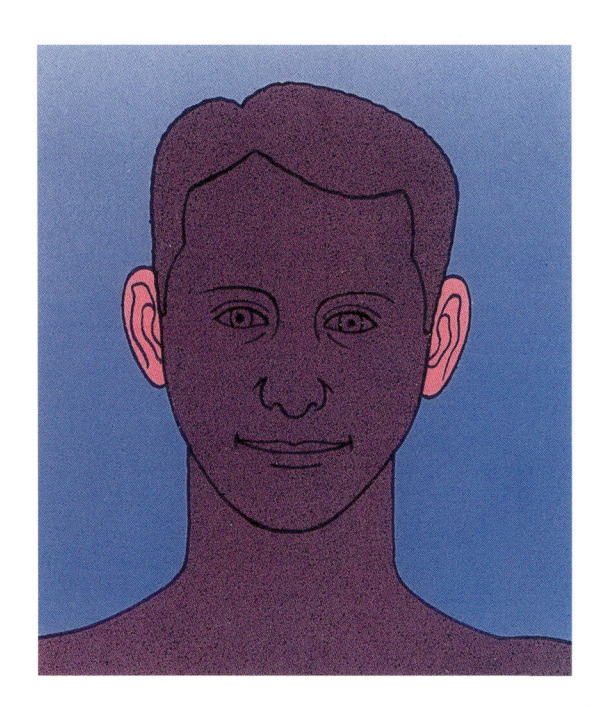

Two fleshy dishes on the sides of your head funnel sound into your ears. These mini-microphones send signals to your brain, letting you hear.

A tape recorder can pick up and store sounds—but your ears and brain are much smarter than this. Together they can make you aware of the sounds around you and enable you to tell what they are.

Sound waves

Things make sounds when they force the air around them to **vibrate**. When a sound reaches your ear, the vibrating air is carried through to a set of **receptors**.

Turn it down!

The receptors inside your ears are covered in delicate hairs that are very easy to damage. Too much loud sound can bend these hairs so much, they snap in half. As broken receptor cells cannot repair themselves, damage from noise usually lasts for life.

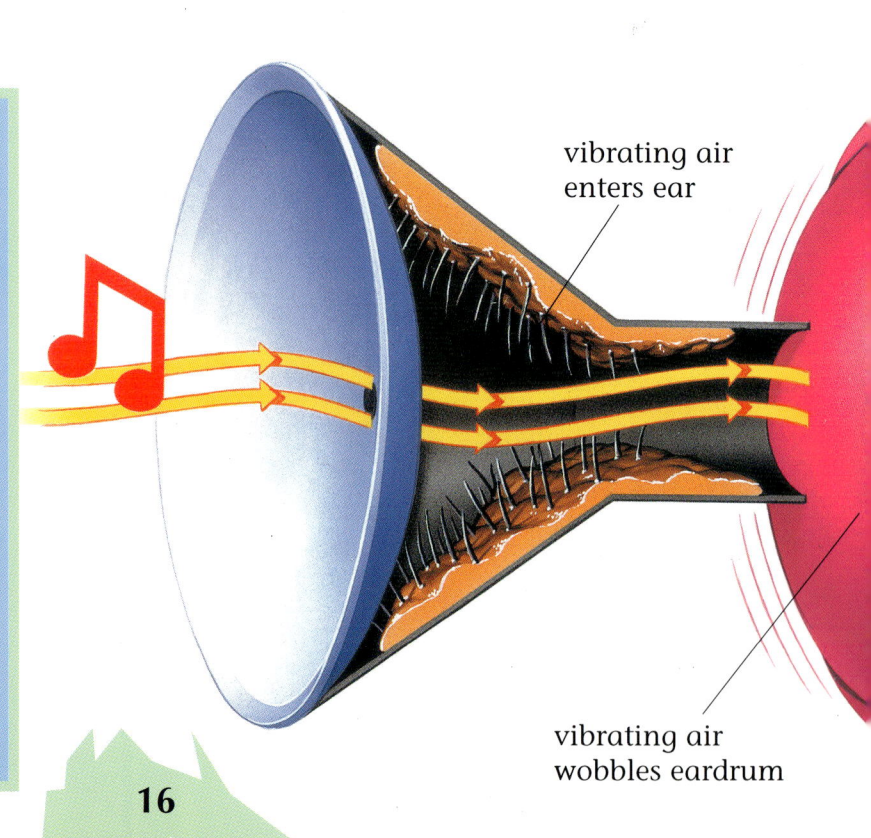

vibrating air enters ear

vibrating air wobbles eardrum

16

Balancing act

As well as letting you hear, your ears help you to balance. Each ear has a set of three tubes, called **semicircular canals**, that are filled with fluid. At the base of each tube is a clump of hairy receptor cells embedded in a jelly. As you move, the fluid inside the tubes forces these hairs to bend. This sends signals to your brain, telling you which way you are moving and which way up you are.

Balance receptor in the ear

fluid inside semicircular canal

movement of fluid bends hairs

receptor hairs

sensory nerve

person moves in this direction

Shaking skin

Inside your ear is a thin, stiff sheet called your **eardrum**. Vibrating air makes the eardrum wobble like a drumskin. As it wobbles, it touches the first in a chain of three tiny bones, called **ossicles**.

semicircular canals help with balance

nerves carry signals to brain

ossicles knock together and shake oval window

fluid inside cochlea ripples

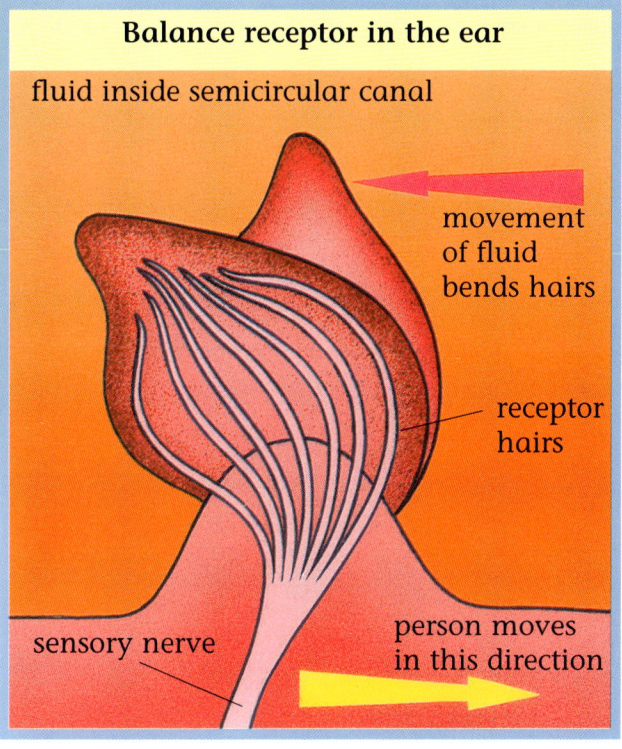

Chain reaction

Your ossicles knock together to pass the vibration deeper into your ear. This wobbles another thin sheet called the **oval window**.

Liquid ripples

Behind the oval window is a spiral tube called the **cochlea**, which is packed with a thick fluid. As the oval window vibrates, it sends ripples through this fluid.

Inside your cochlea is a thin, skin-like sheet that is bristling with hairy receptor **cells**. As the fluid ripples, it bends the hairs. This sends messages along **nerves** to your brain, enabling you to hear and understand the sound.

CHEMICAL TESTERS

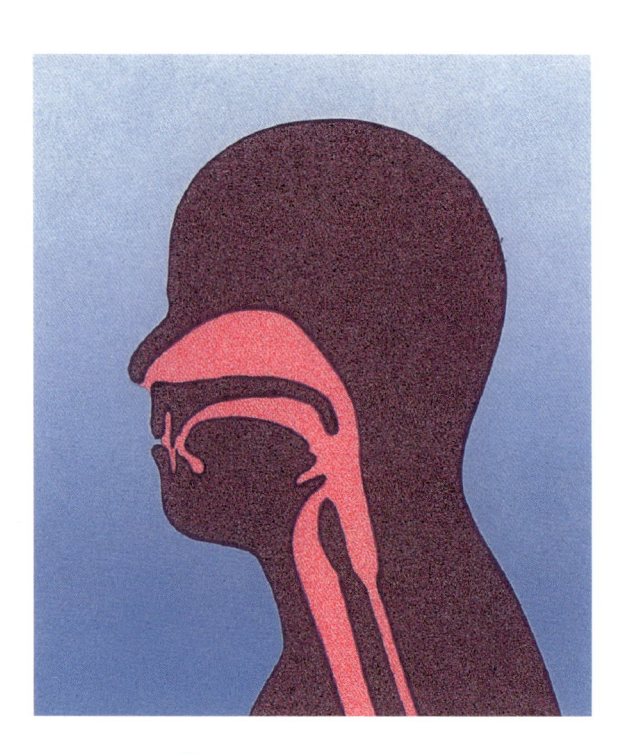

slimy hairs detect smells

A pair of testers—your nose and tongue—help you check you're not taking in anything harmful when you breathe or eat. They're packed with receptors that send messages to your brain whenever they sense chemical changes.

saliva coats tongue and taste buds

Blocked up

When you have a blocked-up nose, it's often hard to tell what you are tasting. That's because your sense of smell helps you to identify many flavors that your taste buds can't detect on their own. If the receptors in your nose become clogged with mucus—when you have a cold, for instance—they stop working so well. This means you pick up far fewer flavors.

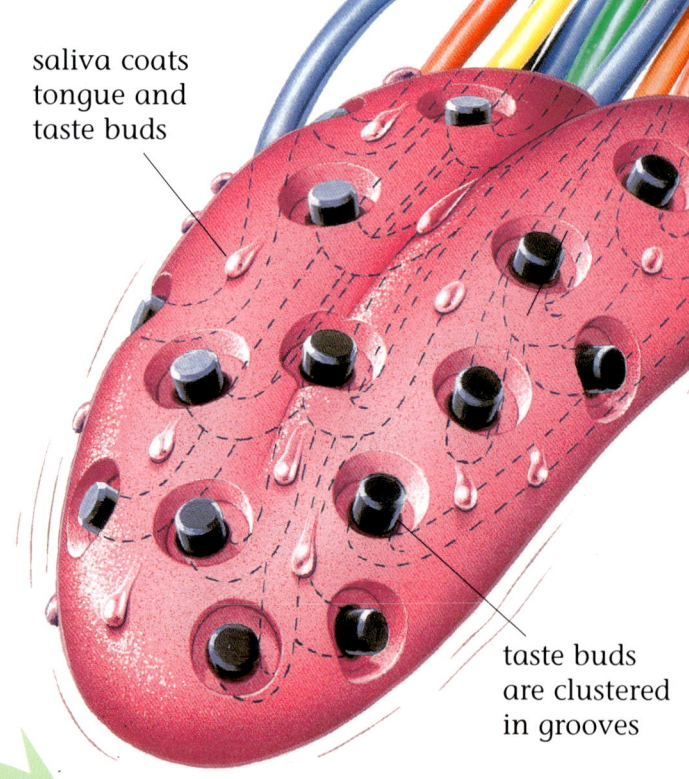

taste buds are clustered in grooves

Taste testers

Your senses of smell and taste are both produced by **chemoreceptors**—**cells** that pick up chemical changes in the liquids sloshing around them.

nerves carry signals to brain

Taste areas on the tongue

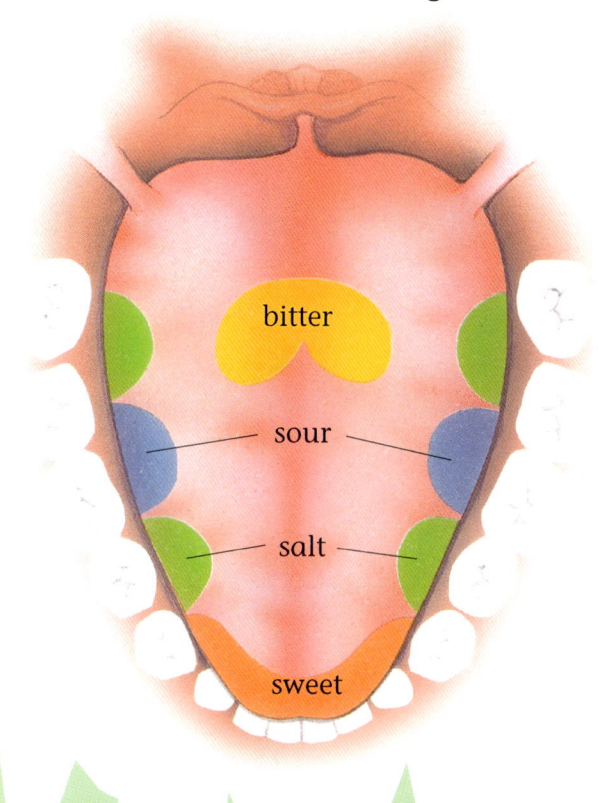

Your mouth has chemoreceptors called **taste buds**. A few of these are scattered around the linings of your cheeks and the roof of your mouth, but most are clustered in tiny circular grooves all over your tongue. Taste buds pick up four main flavors. The tip of your tongue tastes sweet things, the sides taste salt or sour, and the back senses bitter flavors.

bitter
sour
salt
sweet

Loose juice

Inside your mouth is a slimy, watery liquid called **saliva**. This helps you to break down food and bind it into soft balls that you can swallow. Saliva also soaks up sugars, salts, and some other food ingredients. When this mixture sloshes over your taste buds it sets them into action. They send messages to your brain about the flavors they sense.

Smell cells

Deep inside your nose, at the top of your **nasal cavity**, are thousands of smell **receptors**. These hairy cells are bathed in slimy **mucus**, so they're always damp. Some chemicals in the air you breathe dissolve in this mucus and move over the slimy hairs. Your brain uses messages from these chemoreceptors to work out what you are smelling.

Same old smell

A nose can soon get used to a smell. A man may become unaware of the scent of his aftershave, for example, after he has been wearing it for a few minutes. Although the smell is still there, he can hardly sense it because his **nervous system** has stopped processing messages about it.

FINE FEELERS

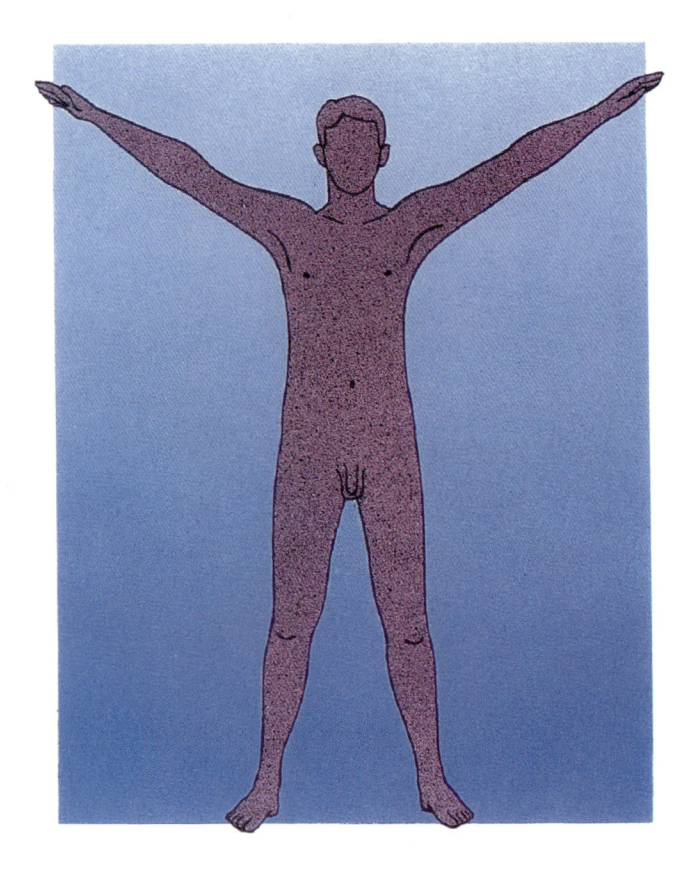

The human machine is covered with receptors that act like built-in feelers. They send messages to your brain when they sense changes in your skin.

There are many different **receptors** in your skin. They tell you when you are touching something, becoming warmer or cooler, feeling pressure, or experiencing pain.

Plain pain

The receptors that make you feel pain are the simplest ones of all. Each one is just a bare **dendrite**. These send messages when they are pressed against, torn, or made too hot or too cold. You have many pain receptors dotted all around your body. These act like alarms, telling you when anything bad is happening to you.

In touch

Other receptors dotted under your skin tell you when you are brushing past something. Your brain also uses their messages to work out the textures of things you touch. Larger receptors that are deeper under your skin help you to feel heavy pressure or vibrations. Others let you feel heat or cold.

tickle triggers touch receptors

receptors send signals along nerves

Receptors in the skin

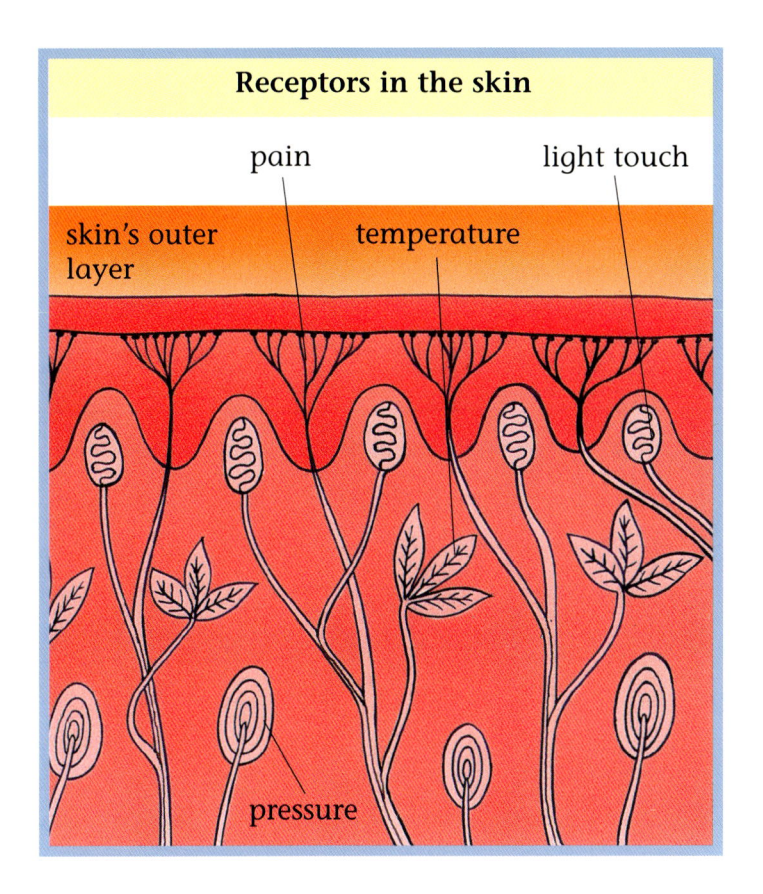

- pain
- light touch
- skin's outer layer
- temperature
- pressure

brain works out what you're touching

nerves carry signals to brain

Muscle messengers

You also have receptors built into your muscles. The messages they send vary as your muscles tighten. Your brain uses these messages to work out how it should change each muscle. In this way, the receptors help you to balance and move around.

How do you know if you are balanced? Find out on page 17.

Sensitive spots

As some parts of your body need to be more sensitive than others, they are packed with more built-in feelers. Your fingertips and the inside of your mouth, for example, have hundreds more receptors than your thighs and back. Body parts with few receptors are not very sensitive at all.

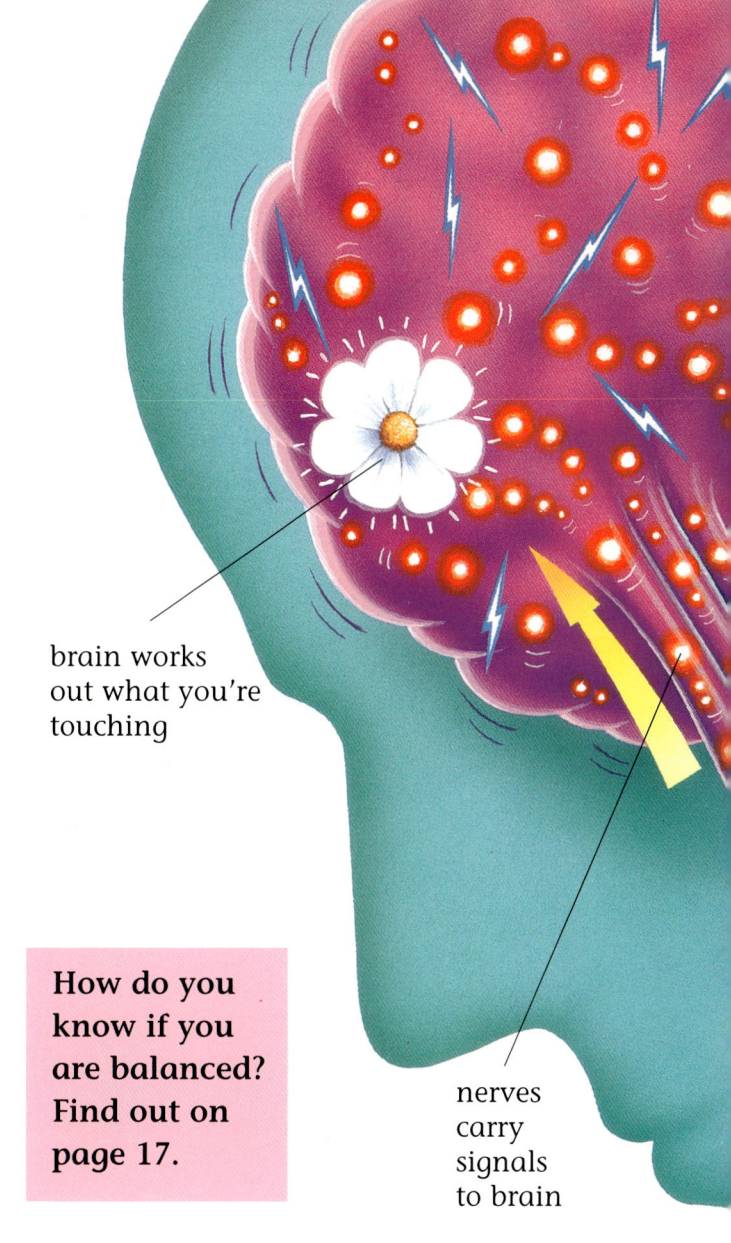

Signal failure

When body parts are very cold, they may feel numb. That's because very little blood runs to them. With this weak blood supply, the **nerves** *and receptors can't get the energy they need to send electrical pulses. But when you warm up, your blood supply usually improves and your feeling returns.*

INFORMATION EXCHANGE

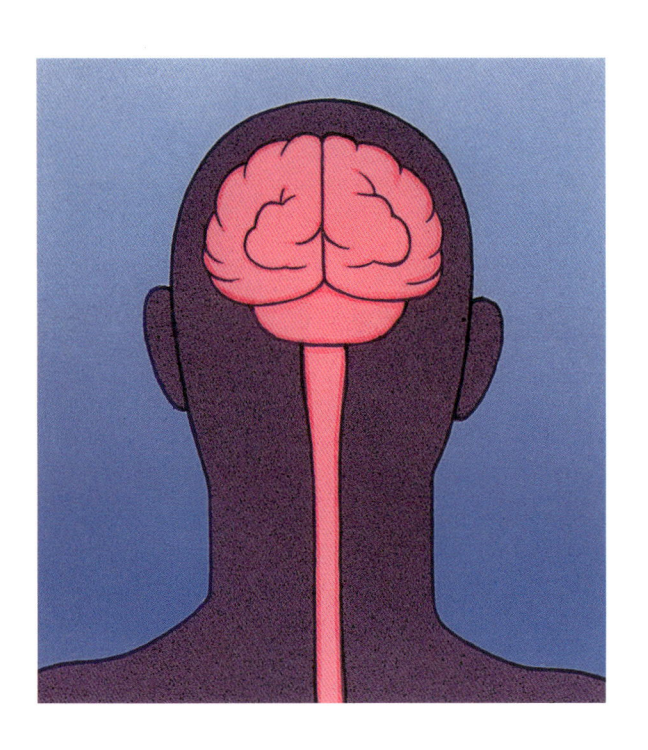

The part of your brain where most thinking goes on is called your cerebrum. Messages from the rest of your body are carefully filtered by your brain stem before they can reach this higher control center.

nerves link two halves of brain

Your mind would be overloaded if you had to think about everything your body does and everything that's going on around you. Luckily your **brain stem** saves you from this problem.

Filtering through

Your brain stem filters the messages entering your **cerebrum**, so that you only become aware of the most important or up-to-date things. This stops your brain from being overrun. When you first put on a sock, for example, you may feel it on your foot. But soon you'll forget it's there. That's because messages from your foot's touch sensors are no longer reaching your cerebrum.

Double-sided

Your cerebrum is divided into two halves, called your **cerebral hemispheres**. The **nerves** that link these hemispheres to the rest of your body cross over in your brain stem. This means that, in general, your left cerebral hemisphere looks after the right side of your body, and your right hemisphere deals with your body's left side.

Split sight

People who damage one side of their brain can experience some confusing problems. A person who has damaged the back of their right cerebral hemisphere, for instance, may not be able to see anything on their left-hand side. Their eyes may be working perfectly, but their brain can't make sense of what they are seeing.

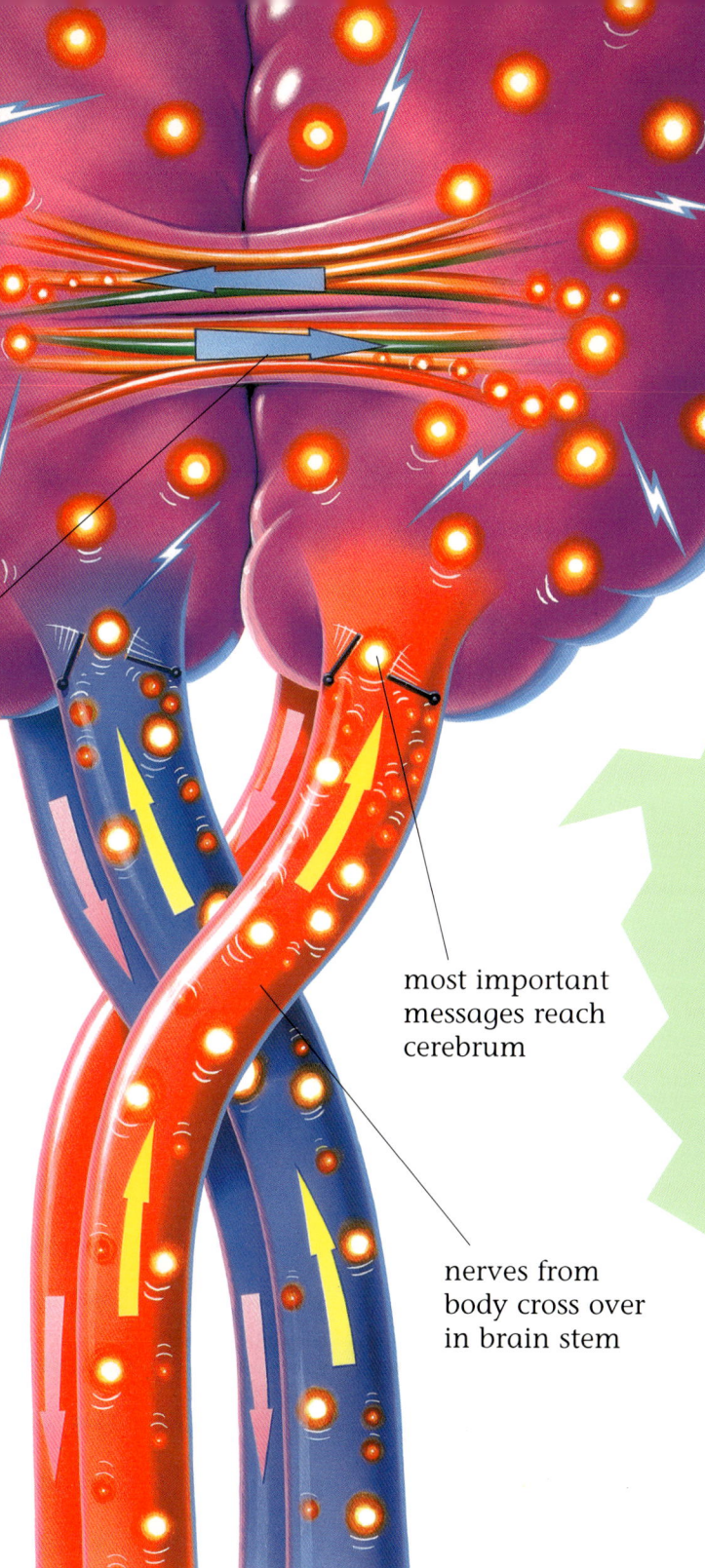

Half and half

Most people use the left half of their brain more than the right half. This is called their **dominant hemisphere**. It's mainly in charge of language, speech, and working out things such as sums. The non-dominant right hemisphere is used more for picturing things and interpreting music and feelings.

most important messages reach cerebrum

nerves from body cross over in brain stem

Left-handers

Left-handed people don't only write differently from right-handers—they may also have different strengths and weaknesses. Unlike the majority of right-handers, most left-handed people have a dominant right hemisphere. This may be why left-handers are often more creative, but slower at learning how to read and spell.

Dominant hemispheres

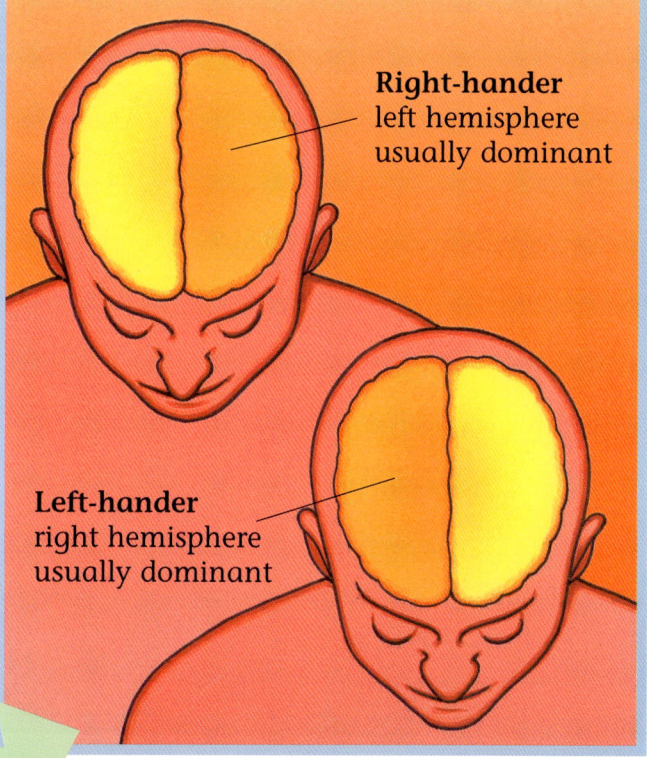

Right-hander left hemisphere usually dominant

Left-hander right hemisphere usually dominant

Linked up

A bundle of nerves, called the **corpus callosum**, connects your two cerebral hemispheres. This enables messages to pass between the two halves of your brain, helping them work together so that you can think clearly and make decisions.

SPECIALIST SECTIONS

Just like the sections in a library, different parts of the human control center deal with different information. Your brain has many specialist areas.

thalamus sorts signals into sections

brain sections control different skills and senses

cerebellum coordinates movement

Sorting system

Your **sensory nerves** are constantly carrying messages to your brain, all about the things you see, hear, feel, and do. You'd get in a terrible muddle if these signals weren't sorted out into some form of order.

A small part of your brain, called the **thalamus**, acts like a switchboard. It monitors the messages coming in and decides which part of the brain they should go to. Your thalamus also gives you a rough idea of whether you are experiencing something nasty or nice.

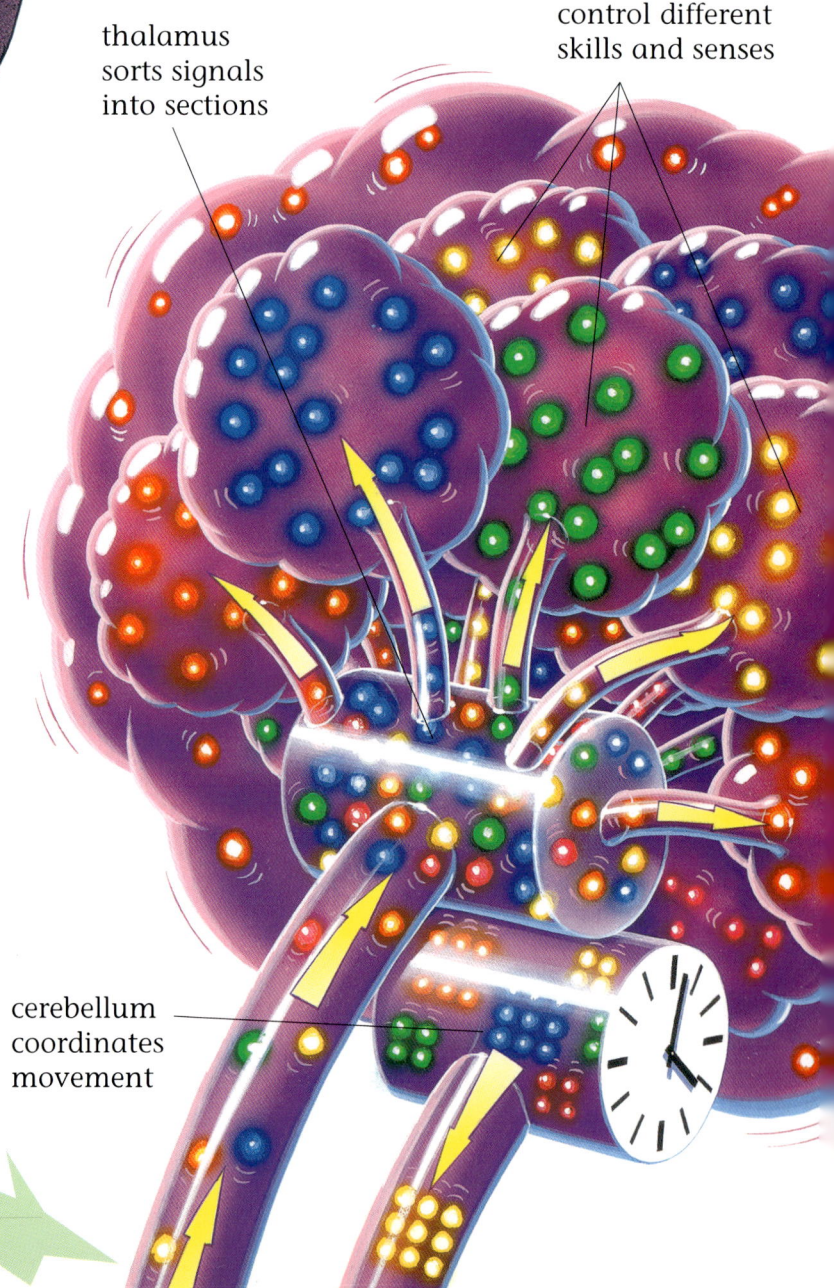

Bad hit

People with severe head injuries may help us to work out what each brain area can do. Some people who have injured a certain spot on the side of their brain, for example, have problems with speaking. They can understand words and they know what they want to say—but they can no longer say it. This shows that the area of brain they have damaged is a place which controls speech.

Expert areas

The main part of your brain that makes you conscious and enables you to think is your **cortex**—the wrinkly outer layer of your **cerebrum**. Each area of your cortex deals with certain thoughts, feelings, and actions.

Sight, for instance, is mainly handled at the back of your brain, touch, movement, and speech at the center, and concentration at the front. A small part of your lower cortex, called the **hippocampus**, is thought to store memories.

Feel good factor

Feelings such as thirst, fear, hunger, and pleasure drive you to act in ways that help you to survive. When you're hungry, for example, you look for more food so you can top up your body's energy supply. These feelings are all controlled and created by an area of your brain called the **limbic system**.

Fine-tuning

Tucked underneath the back of your cerebrum is a small brain section called your **cerebellum**. This helps you to be coordinated. It makes sure you move smoothly and in the right direction by monitoring signals from balance **receptors** in your ear. Messages leaving your brain are put into order by your cerebellum on their way to the rest of your body.

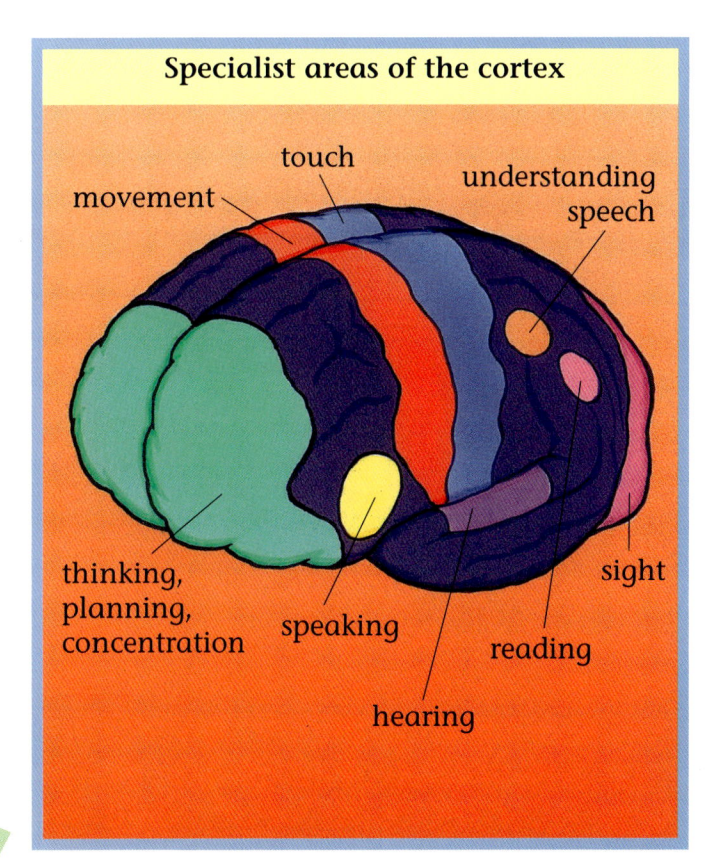

Specialist areas of the cortex

- movement
- touch
- understanding speech
- thinking, planning, concentration
- speaking
- hearing
- reading
- sight

CARE AND SERVICING

A desktop computer is usually out of date after just a few years. But the human control center is always developing, adapting, and making new connections. That's why, if you care for your brain, it can last a lifetime—and why the more you use it, the better it can get.

Playing safe

Even when you are an adult, your brain can adapt, changing the connections inside it as you experience the world and learn. But it can rarely repair itself if it suffers lots of damage. That's why it's important to fully protect your head if you are going to put it in any danger. It's a good idea to wear a helmet, for example, if you go biking or rollerblading.

Out for the count

A bad blow to someone's head can give them **concussion**. This makes them unconscious for a short period of time. When they recover, they may not remember anything about their accident.

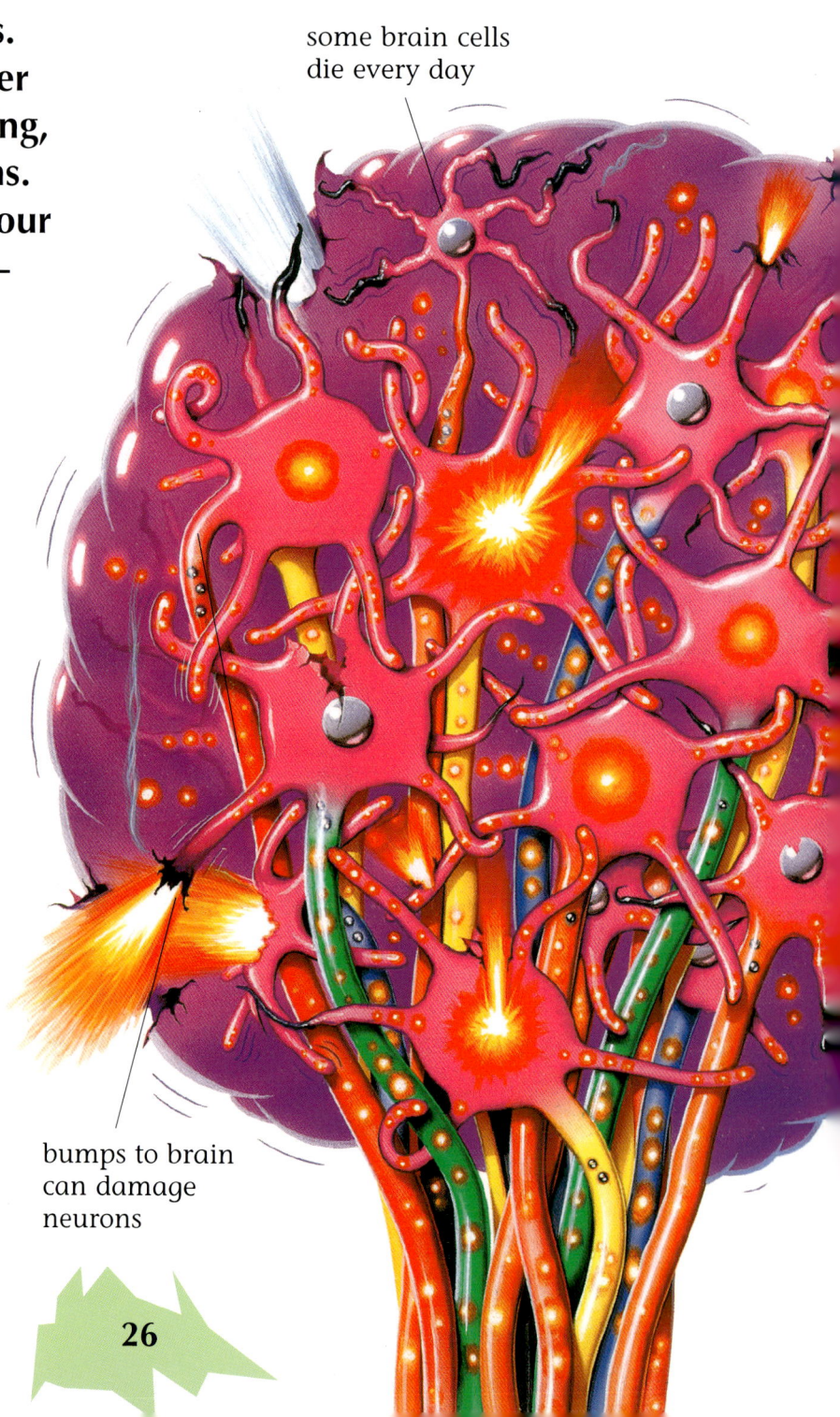

some brain cells die every day

bumps to brain can damage neurons

Losing matter

You are born with all the **neurons** your brain will ever have. As you grow up they become bigger and make more connections. But from early adulthood onward, thousands of neurons die every day, so your brain gradually shrinks in size. There's usually no need to worry about dying neurons. It can take 50 years or more to lose enough to notice, unless you have a brain-destroying disease such as **Alzheimer's**.

Brain cross-sections

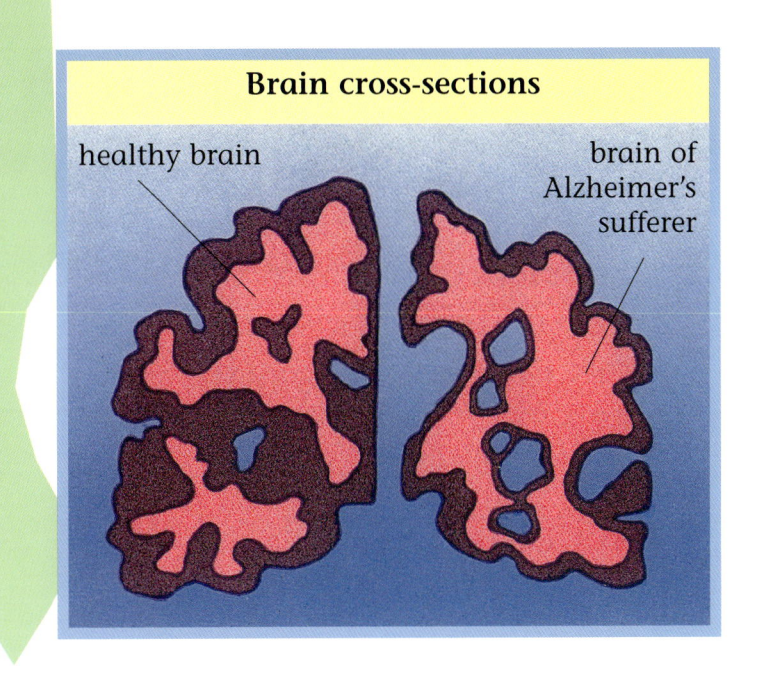

healthy brain

brain of Alzheimer's sufferer

Sound sleep

Sleep is very important for your brain, even though it never rests completely. When you're asleep your brain produces different electrical pulses from when you are awake. That's why you dream. The chemicals that your brain needs to function are replenished when you sleep too.

Getting hooked

Drugs, including alcohol, can seriously harm the **cells** in your brain. Very **addictive** drugs, such as cocaine, do the most damage. They switch on an area deep in the **hypothalamus** which creates feelings of pleasure. When these feelings go away, users need more of the drug to bring the enjoyment back again. But the drug can cause damage to part of the brain, so they may find it hard to be happy again.

Where does it hurt?

When parts of your body are poorly, they often feel sore. But sometimes a completely different part of you may hurt. A shooting pain through your left arm and shoulder, for example, could be a sign of heart trouble. That's because your heart and left arm share some links to your brain. This diagram shows some of the areas where pain may be felt when parts of your body are damaged or unwell.

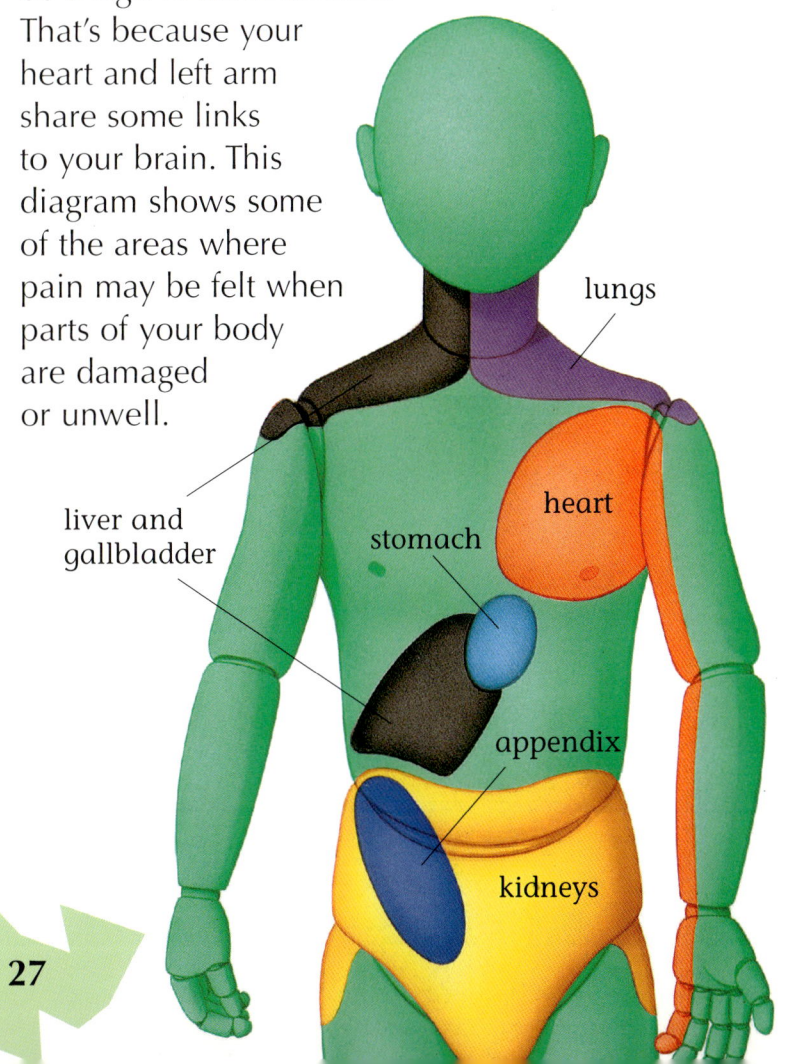

lungs

liver and gallbladder

stomach

heart

appendix

kidneys

27

OTHER MODELS

The human machine may have the most complex controls in the animal kingdom, but many creatures have much sharper senses than we do. Here are just a few of the interesting control systems that are around.

Super senses

We use far more of our brain for seeing than for smelling. But some animals have a different balance between their senses. Dogs, for example, don't see as well as we do, but they have far more sensitive noses. Police often train dogs to sniff out drugs or missing people. Cats have very sensitive eyes and ears, enabling them to hunt at night. Cats and dogs have whiskers that act as simple feelers.

whiskers act as feelers

dogs have strong sense of smell and taste

cats have very good eyesight and hearing

whiskers act as feelers

Rare receptors

Some animals have very different ways of sensing the world around them. Snakes and owls, for instance, rely on special **receptors** which pick up the body heat of their prey. That way they can tell if any food is nearby, even when it's dark. Many insects which feed on blood can also sense the warmth of other animals —they feel it using special bristly hairs.

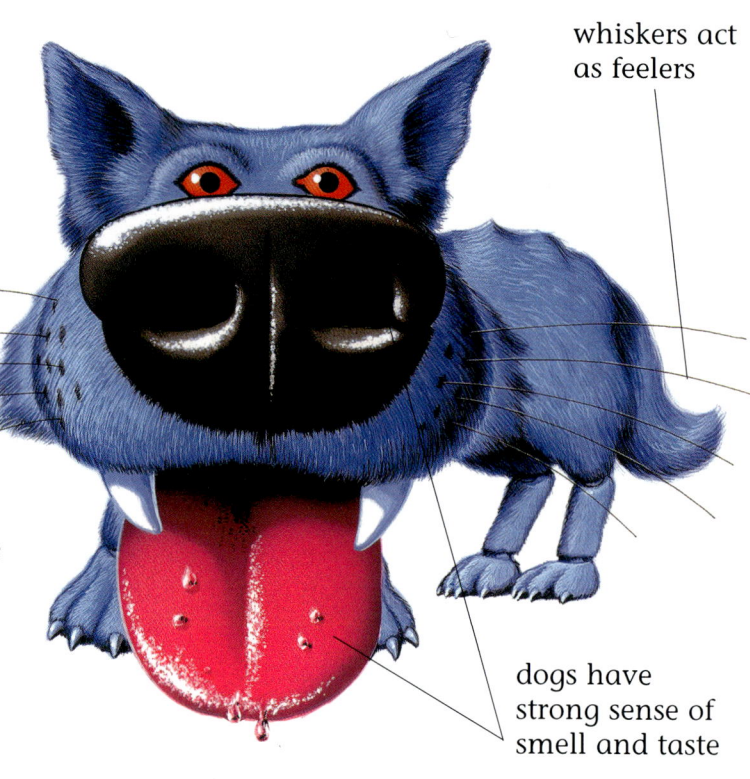

Sound system

Bats have terrible eyesight, so they use their excellent hearing to work out what's going on around them. Bats send out high-pitched squeaks, then listen for any echoes that come back. They use the echoes to work out the size and position of anything in their path.

bat sends out high-pitched sound

echo returns from object nearby

Sizing up

A whale's brain can be twice the size of a human's—but that doesn't mean whales are cleverer than we are. Compared to the rest of a whale's body, its brain is actually very small.

The size of each part of the brain varies from creature to creature. A chimpanzee's **cerebrum** is the closest to ours in size. That's why chimps seem to be so intelligent, acting like humans in many ways. Cats have a relatively large **cerebellum**. This gives them good balance and coordination.

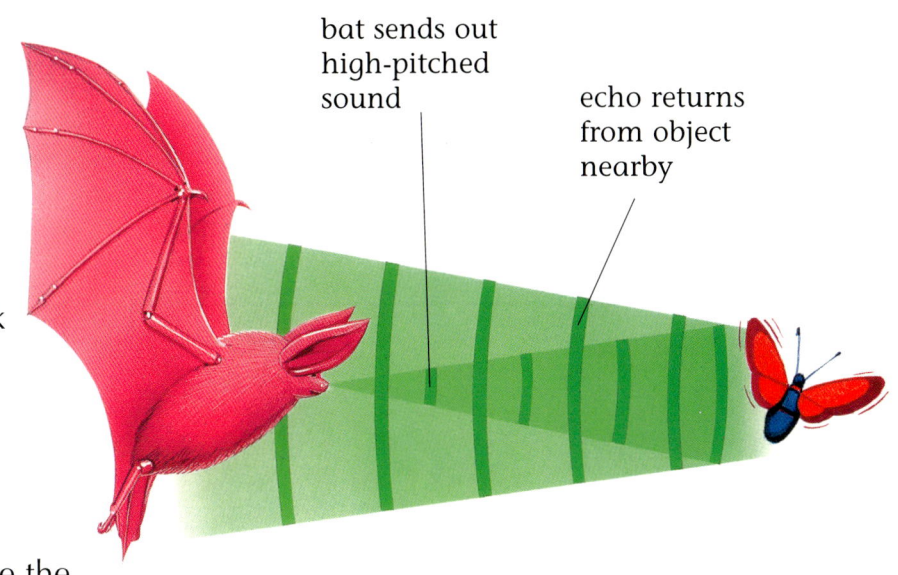

Storing up

Humans may have the most intelligent brains, but some animals can perform feats of memory that we would find very hard to match. A bird called a Clark's nutcracker, for example, buries food for the winter in hundreds of different places. It always remembers exactly where these places are. Very few of us could remember that much information without writing it down.

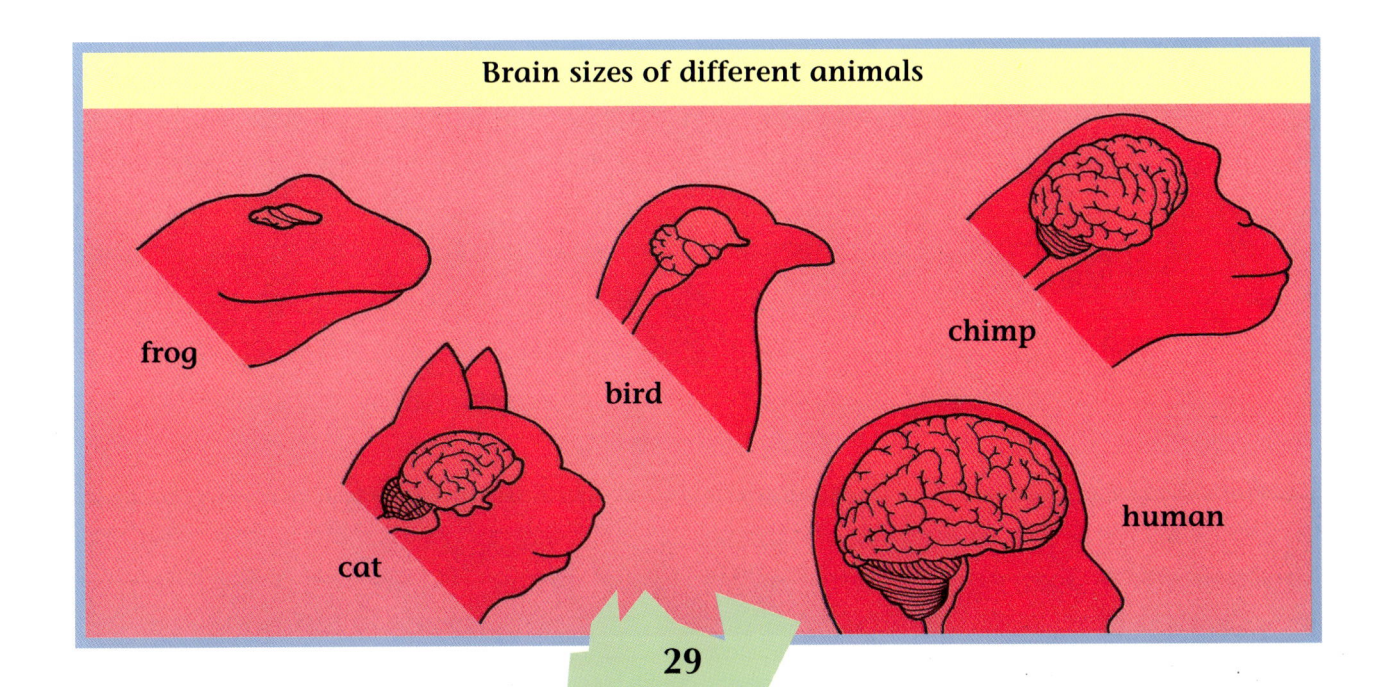

Brain sizes of different animals

frog

bird

chimp

cat

human

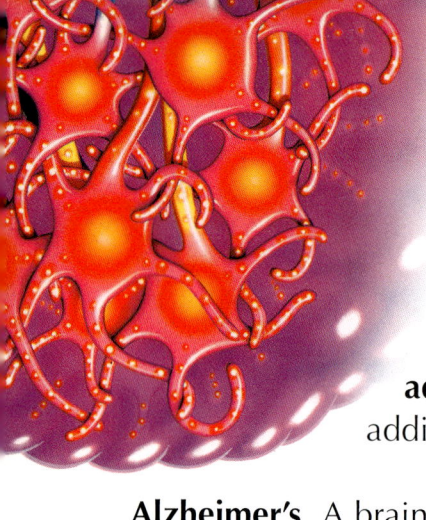

GLOSSARY

addictive Something addictive is hard to give up.

Alzheimer's A brain disease that affects the memory, thinking, and coordination.

anesthetics Drugs that numb the body by stopping nerve signals reaching the brain.

autonomic nervous system A part of the nervous system that runs automatic actions.

axon A fiber, leading from a neuron body, that carries signals to other nerve cells.

brain stem The stalk that links your brain to your spinal cord.

capillaries Tiny blood-carrying tubes.

cells The billions of very tiny parts that combine to make tissues in your body.

cerebellum The part of your brain, under the cerebrum, that coordinates your movement.

cerebral hemispheres The two (left and right) halves of your cerebrum.

cerebrum The main part of your brain that deals with conscious thought and feelings.

chemoreceptors Receptor cells that detect chemicals.

cochlea The hollow, spiral bone in your ear.

concussion Damage to the brain, causing temporary loss of consciousness.

corpus callosum The bundle of nerves that joins your two cerebral hemispheres.

cortex The outer part of your cerebrum.

dendrites Fibers that bring a neuron signals from other nerve cells.

dominant hemisphere The half of your brain that you use the most.

eardrum A thin sheet inside your ear that vibrates when sound waves hit it.

fibers Fine strands that make up many parts of your body, including your nerves.

gray matter The mass of neuron bodies that forms the outer part of your cerebrum and the center of your spinal cord.

hippocampus A part of your brain that controls memory and learning.

hormones Chemical messengers that tell parts of your body when and how to work.

hypothalamus A part of your brain that monitors conditions inside your body and helps to keep them stable.

iris The ring of muscle around your pupil. It forms the colored part of your eye.

lens The transparent sack of fluid that bends light rays as they enter your eye.

limbic system A brain region that controls emotions and behavior.

motor nerves Nerves carrying messages from your brain to the rest of your body.

mucus The slime that lines your nose, airways, and digestive tubes.

multiple sclerosis A disease that attacks the coating around nerve cells.

nasal cavity The hollow behind your nose.

nerves Fine threads that carry messages between your brain and other body parts.

nervous system The network of nerves all around your body, including your brain.

neuroglia Cells that support your neurons.

neurons The cells that transmit electrical pulses through your brain and nerves.

neurotransmitters Chemicals that carry electrical pulses across a synapse.

nutrients The chemical substances in food that your body needs to survive.

optic nerves Nerves that link your eyes to your brain.

ossicles The three tiny bones inside each ear—the smallest bones in your body.

oval window A tiny skin-like sheet which passes sound waves into your cochlea.

oxygen A gas in the air that you breathe. Your body cells need it to work properly.

pituitary gland A tiny part at the base of your brain that produces hormones.

pupil The hole at the center of your eye.

receptors Cells that sense changes in and around your body.

reflex An action that you do automatically.

retina The lining at the back of your eye that is sensitive to light.

saliva The juice inside your mouth.

sedative Something that makes you sleepy.

semicircular canals Curving tubes inside your ear which contain balance receptors.

sense organs Parts of your body which you use to detect changes around you.

sensory nerves Nerves which carry signals from receptors to your brain.

spinal cord The main bundle of nerves that runs down your spine.

synapse The tiny gap that signals pass through from one neuron to another.

taste buds Receptors inside your mouth that pick up flavors.

thalamus A brain region which sorts out messages coming in from your sense organs.

vibrate To wobble very quickly to and fro.

white matter The mass of axons that makes up the outer part of your spinal cord and the inside of your brain.

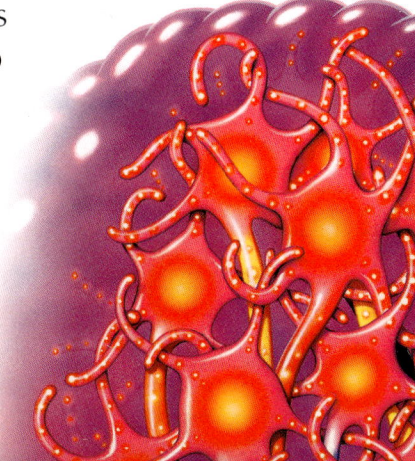

INDEX

addiction 27, 30
Alzheimer's disease 27, 30
anesthetics 7, 30
autonomic nervous system
      12, 13, 30
axons 9, 30, 31

balance 17, 21, 25, 29, 31
brain 4, 5, 6, 7, 8, 9, 10,
      11, 12, 14, 15, 16,
      17, 18, 19, 20, 21,
      22, 23, 24, 25, 26,
      27, 28, 29, 30, 31
brain stem 12, 13, 22, 30

capillaries 7, 30
cells 4, 7, 9, 10, 14, 16, 17,
      19, 27, 30, 31
cerebellum 25, 29, 30
cerebrum 6, 7, 22, 23, 25,
      29, 30
chemoreceptors 19, 30
cochlea 17, 30, 31
color blindness 15
concussion 26, 30
coordination 25, 29, 30
corpus callosum 23, 30
cortex 7, 25, 30

dendrites 9, 20, 30

ears 16-17, 28, 30, 31
eardrum 17, 30
eyes 12, 14-15, 22, 28,
      30, 31

fibers 4, 7, 8, 9, 10, 30
fluid 6, 9, 17, 30

gray matter 7, 10, 12, 30

hearing 16-17, 24, 29
heart 12, 13, 27
hippocampus 25, 30
hormones 13, 30, 31
hypothalamus 13, 27, 30

intelligence 29
iris 14, 30

language 23, 25
learning 5, 9, 23, 26, 30
left-handedness 23
lens 15, 30
limbic system 25, 30
lungs 12, 27

memory 6, 8, 9, 25, 26,
      29, 30
motor nerves 10, 31
moving 4, 5, 11, 13, 15, 17,
      21, 25, 30
multiple sclerosis 11, 31
muscles 11, 14, 15, 21

nerves 4, 8, 9, 10, 11, 12, 13,
      17, 21, 22, 23, 30, 31
nervous system 4, 5, 10, 11,
      12, 19, 30, 31
neuroglia 7, 31
neurons 4, 6, 7, 8, 9, 10,
      11, 14, 27, 30, 31
neurotransmitters 9, 31
numbness 8, 11, 21, 30
nutrients 7, 31

optic nerves 14, 31

ossicles 17, 31
oval window 17, 31
oxygen 7, 31

pain 20, 27
pituitary gland 13, 31
pupils 12, 14, 31

receptors 4, 10, 11, 14, 15,
      16, 17, 18, 19, 20, 21,
      25, 28, 31
reflexes 11, 12, 14, 15, 31
retina 15, 31

sedatives 8, 31
seeing 5, 14-15, 22, 24, 25,
      28, 29
semicircular canals 17, 31
sense organs 4, 14, 31
sensory nerves 10, 24, 31
sleep 6, 8, 13, 27
smelling 18-19, 28
speech 5, 23, 25
spinal cord 10, 11, 12, 30, 31
stress 13
synapse 9, 31

taste 18-19
taste buds 18, 19, 31
temperature 13, 20
thalamus 24, 31
thinking 4, 6, 8, 12, 22,
      23, 25, 30
tongue 18, 19
touch 11, 20, 21, 22, 25

white matter 7, 10, 31

32

PROPERTY OF
MULGRAVE SCHOOL
LIBRARY